PREFACE

This publication is part of a series produced by the Institute's staff through use of the Institute's National Automated Accounting Research System (NAARS). The purpose of the series is to provide interested readers with examples of the application of technical pronouncements. It is believed that those who are confronted with problems in the application of pronouncements can benefit from seeing how others apply them in practice.

It is the intention to publish periodically similar compilations of information of current interest dealing with aspects of financial reporting.

The examples presented were selected from over twenty thousand annual reports stored in the NAARS computer data base.

This compilation presents only a limited number of examples and is not intended to encompass all aspects of the application of the pronouncements covered in this survey. Individuals with special application problems not illustrated in the survey may arrange for special computer searches of the NAARS data banks by contacting the Institute.

The views expressed are solely those of the staff.

John Graves
Director, Technical Services

TABLE OF CONTENTS

I

SCOPE AND PURPOSE OF THE SURVEY

Although authoritative literature exists in this area, the accounting profession recently decided to restudy the accounting procedures for quasi-reorganizations. The reasons for the restudy, the various issues involved, and the arguments for and against the accounting on each issue are presented in Issues Paper 88-1, *Quasi-Reorganizations*, issued September 22, 1988, by the AICPA Accounting Standards Division. Not all of the alternative methods presented and criteria described in the issues paper necessarily comply with generally accepted accounting principles. Therefore, the issues paper, reproduced as appendix C herein, is not intended to provide guidance on the preferability of accounting principles.

In addition, the AICPA Accounting Standards Division plans soon to report on and provide guidance for issues of entities in reorganization and entities emerging from reorganization proceedings.

This survey primarily is intended to show how entities have been applying quasi-reorganizations in practice. It is not intended to provide guidance on the preferability or the acceptability of accounting principles or disclosure requirements.

TWO ACCOUNTING PROCEDURES

The Issues Paper uses the term *quasi-reorganization* to denote two accounting procedures. The first procedure consists of reclassifying a deficit in retained earnings as a reduction of additional paid-in capital. The second procedure consists of such a reclassification in addition to a restatement of the carrying amounts of assets with or without a restatement of the carrying amounts of liabilities. Adoption of either procedure is approved by the authoritative accounting literature quoted in the Issues Paper. The Issues Paper also presents the various views of the two procedures that have been expressed by accountants.

DEFICIT RECLASSIFICATION ONLY

Accountants disagree as to whether a deficit reclassification alone should ever be permitted. Accountants who would permit deficit reclassifications would do so partly to allow enterprises that are prohibited by state laws from paying dividends because of deficits in retained earnings to pay them. Those accountants believe legal prohibitions on paying dividends that could otherwise be paid cause unnecessary hardship for many stockholders. Accountants who would not permit deficit reclassifications would not do so partly because they contend that retained earnings is a useful statistic, the integrity of which should be protected.

Some accountants who would permit deficit reclassifications would permit them only if one or more of the following conditions are met:

- The enterprise must demonstrate a reasonable prospect of future profitability.
- The enterprise must demonstrate that circumstances of operation have changed.
- The deficit must have resulted from net losses other than preoperating, start-up, or development-stage losses.
- The deficit must not have resulted from the subtraction from retained earnings of dividends or amounts resulting from transactions in the enterprise's own stock.
- The reclassification must be approved by the enterprise's stockholders.
- A reasonable determination must be made that retained earnings that would be reported subsequent to the reclassification would support payment of dividends under state law.
- The enterprise whose deficit is to be reclassified must not be a wholly owned subsidiary unless the parent company records its own deficit reclassification.

DEFICIT RECLASSIFICATION COMBINED WITH RESTATEMENT

Accountants also disagree as to whether a deficit reclassification in combination with a restatement of assets with or without a restatement of liabilities should ever be permitted. Some accountants who would permit the combination would permit it only if one or more of the conditions described above are met. Other accountants would permit it only if total equity would not be negative after restatement. Others would permit it only if restatement would not result in an increase in total equity.

In accomplishing the restatement, some accountants would restate all the assets of the enterprise, and others would restate only assets for which there is evidence of impairment. Some would additionally restate liabilities and others would not. Some would recognize goodwill and others would not. Some would restate assets to current fair values, but others would restate them to the undiscounted or discounted net future cash flows the assets are expected to generate.

SOURCE OF ILLUSTRATIONS

Application of quasi-reorganizations consistent with existing authoritative accounting literature requires considerable judgment. An accountant confronted with problems in applying a quasi-reorganization can benefit from learning how other accountants are applying it in practice. Accordingly, this publication presents excerpts from recently published financial statements of fifty-one companies that illustrate its application. The AICPA National Automated Accounting Research System (NAARS) was used to compile the information. The examples presented herein were selected from the 1983/84, 1984/85, 1985/86, 1986/87, and 1987/88 annual report files.

ASSETS NOT RESTATED—RESTATEMENT SAID TO BE UNNECESSARY

As discussed in chapter 1, the companies that applied quasi-reorganizations differed principally in that some of the companies restated assets while other companies did not. Of those companies that did not restate assets, some said that restatement was unnecessary because the fair values of their assets equalled the carrying values at the times of the quasi-reorganizations. Seven examples of such companies are presented below. One of the companies restated liabilities without restating assets. The examples are classified according to whether the company was or was not being reorganized in a bankruptcy proceeding at the time of the quasi-reorganization.

NOT UNDER BANKRUPTCY PROCEEDING

ASTROTECH INTERNATIONAL CORPORATION AND SUBSIDIARIES

Consolidated Balance Sheet (Operating Company)
(in thousands except per share)

	September 30, 1984
Common Stockholders' Equity:	
Common Stock, $.30 par value, authorized 80,000,000 shares; issued and outstanding 40,108,723 shares	12,033
Additional capital	7,498
Retained earnings since September 30, 1984*	19,531
Total Liabilities and Stockholders' Equity	$142,818

*Deficit as of September 30, 1984, eliminated in quasi-reorganization $28,260.

• • • •

Consolidated Statement of Common Stockholders' Equity (Operating Company)
(in thousands except per share)

| | Eleven Months Ended September 30, 1984 | | |
	Common Stock	Additional Capital	Retained Earnings (Deficit)
Balance at November 1, 1983, as restated	$10,314	26,581	$(24,607)
Net loss			(1,517)
Sale of 5,729,817 common shares at $2.00 per share	1,719	9,742	
Dividends to preferred shareholders			(1,874)
Accretion of preferred stock redemption requirement			(262)
Effect of quasi-reorganization as of September 30, 1984		(28,825)	28,260
Balance at September 30, 1984	$12,033	$ 7,498	$ 0

Notes to Financial Statements
September 30, 1984
(in thousands except per share)

• • • •

10. Quasi-Reorganization

In connection with the Company's change in character from an investment company to an operating company, the Board of Directors approved a Corporate re-adjustment of the accounts as of September 30, 1984, effected in accordance with accounting principles applicable to quasi-reorganizations. This action does not require shareholder approval under Delaware law.

Because substantially all the assets and liabilities of the Company have been recently recorded at their fair values in connection with acquisitions accounted for using the purchase method of accounting, and nothing has occurred since then to indicate a material change in such values, the Company determined that no adjustment to carrying values was necessary. The carrying value of the redeemable preferred stock has been increased to reflect its market value at September 30, 1984.

The quasi-reorganization has been accomplished by offsetting the increase in carrying value of the preferred stock of $565 and the accumulated deficit in retained earnings of $28,260 against the additional capital account.

BURKHART PETROLEUM CORPORATION

Consolidated Balance Sheets
December 31, 1985 and 1984

	1985	1984
Common stockholders' equity (Notes 3 and 12):		
Common stock—$.01 par value; 40,000,000 shares authorized; 5,770,929 shares issued and outstanding in 1985	57	
Common stock—$1 par value; 500,000 shares authorized; 101,650 shares issued and outstanding in 1984	101	
Capital in excess of par value	1,596	188
Accumulated deficit		(8,096)
Total common stockholders' equity	1,654	(7,806)

• • • •

Consolidated Statement of Changes in Common Stockholders' Equity

| | Common Stock | | | |
	$1 Par Value Amount	$.01 Par Value Amount	Capital in Excess of Par Value	Accumulated Deficit
Balance, December 31, 1984	101		188	(8,096)
Net loss for the year ended December 31, 1985				(1,117)
Business combination and quasi-reorganization (Note 3):				
Acquisition of Henderson Petroleum Corporation		20	240	
Conversion of Burkhart $1 par value common stock	(101)	9	91	
Conversion of redeemable preferred stock		27	11,044	
Quasi-Reorganization			(9,214)	9,214
Stock registration, issuance and associated costs			(754)	
Balance, December 31, 1985	0	$57	$ 1,596	0

Notes to Consolidated Financial Statements

• • • •

Note 3. Business Combination and Quasi-Reorganization

The merger of Burkhart and Henderson was effective on December 31, 1985, pursuant to a plan and agreement of merger dated August 29, 1985, which was approved by the respective groups of stockholders on December 17, 1985. In connection with the merger, Burkhart's common stockholders converted 101,650 shares of Burkhart $1 par value common stock and Henderson's common stock-holders converted 8,079,300 shares of Henderson $ .01 par value common stock into 989,882 and 2,019,825 shares, respectively, of the Company's $ .01 par value common stock. In addition, the holders of Burkhart's no par value Preferred Stock, Series A, and 10 percent Cumulative Convertible Preferred Stock, Series B, converted 30,000 and 118,000 shares, respectively, of redeemable preferred stock into 581,455 and 2,179,767 shares, respectively, of the Company's $ .01 par value common stock. The merger was accounted for as an acquisition of Henderson by Burkhart, under the purchase method of accounting for business combinations.

• • • •

In connection with the merger, the Company's stockholders approved a quasi-reorganization, which resulted in the transfer of Burkhart's accumulated deficit in retained earnings of $9,214,173 to capital in excess of par value. Other than the elimination of accumulated depreciation, depletion and amortization against property and equipment accounts, no adjustments were made to the assets and liabilities at December 31, 1985, in connection with the quasi-reorganization since historical book values of Burkhart's assets and liabilities approximated estimated fair values.

In connection with effecting the business combination and quasi-reorganization, the Company incurred costs of $754,598 which were charged against capital in excess of par value. Those costs include $151,809 payable to a company controlled by a person who was a Director of both Burkhart and Henderson and who is a Director of the Company, for financial advisory services provided in connection with arranging the merger.

• • • •

PRINCEVILLE DEVELOPMENT CORPORATION

Consolidated Balance Sheet

	November 15, 1984 Before Pushdown Adjustment
Stockholders' equity (Notes 1, 10 and 13):	
Common stock, 25,000,000 shares of $0.20 par value authorized;	
8,740,000 shares issued and outstanding	1,748
Capital surplus at November 15, 1984	53,702
Retained earnings (deficit) at November 15, 1984	3,582[a]
Total stockholders' equity	59,033

[a]After quasi-reorganization on December 1, 1983.

Notes to Consolidated Financial Statements

• • • •

10. Capital Stock:

• • • •

Princeville Development Corporation (a wholly owned subsidiary of Consolidated Oil & Gas, Inc.) at November 15, 1984:

Effective December 1, 1983, the shareholder of the subsidiary approved a quasi-reorganization. This resulted in a reclassification of the accumulated deficit of $11,937,666 at November 30, 1983, to capital surplus. In the opinion of management, there was no indication of impairment of its assets at that date which would have required their writedown in conjunction with the quasi-reorganization.

UNDER BANKRUPTCY PROCEEDING

REGENCY AFFILIATES, INC. AND SUBSIDIARIES

Consolidated Balance Sheet

	December 31, 1987
Stockholders' equity (deficit) (notes 1 and 6):	

• • • •

Common stock of $.40 par value. Authorized 25,000,000 shares; issued and outstanding 3,714,525 shares	1,485
Deficit	(1,670)
Treasury stock, 8,711 shares, at cost	(23)
Total stockholders' deficit	(208)

Notes to Consolidated Balance Sheet

1. Business and Reorganization

Regency Affiliates, Inc. (RAI or the Company), formerly Transcontinental Energy Corporation (TEC), a public company with 3,900 shareholders, was previously engaged in the onshore contract drilling of oil and gas wells and the exploration for and production of crude oil and natural gas in several states. The Company comprised several subsidiaries and partnerships prior to a filing for reorganization in October 1984 under Chapter 11 of the Bankruptcy Act.

Efforts to reorganize its oil and gas business ultimately failed and, as a result, the Company filed a liquidation plan with the court which plan was later modified (Modified Plan) and approved by the creditors and stockholders in September 1986. The implementation of the Modified Plan resulted in the reorganization of the Company as of December 30, 1987. The Company is not resuming its oil and natural gas business, but instead intends to acquire established profitable companies with ongoing management.

• • • •

A corporate readjustment of the accounts as of December 30, 1987 was effected in accordance with accounting principles applicable to a quasi-reorganization. The Company determined that no adjustment to carrying values was necessary as the assets and liabilities were nominal and their recorded accounting values approximate fair value.

Following is a summary of the reorganization private offering and corporate readjustment transactions:

	Common Stock		Additional Paid-In Capital	Deficit	Treasury Stock
	$.10 par	$.40 par			
Balances before reorganization	$804,890		$ 73,331,082	$(101,721,017)	$(23,302)
Reorganization and related transactions:					
Exchange of $.10 par value shares for $.40 par value shares	(804,890)	$804,890			
Issuance of 747,500 shares common stock in satisfaction of creditors' claims		299,000	27,252,019		
Reorganization costs			(343,785)		
Sale of 50 Units of private offering— representing 954,800 shares		381,920	53,333		
Private offering costs			(242,228)		
Corporate readjustment of capital accounts			(100,050,421)	100,050,421	
Balances at December 31, 1987			$ 1,485,810	$ (1,670,596)	$(23,302)

• • • •

TACOMA BOATBUILDING CO.

Balance Sheets
(in thousands)

	December 31	
	1987	1986
Stockholders' equity (deficiency in assets):		
• • • •		
New Common Stock, $.01 par value: Authorized: 100,000,000 shares; Issued: 60,689,655 shares	607	
Old Common Stock, $1.00 par value: Authorized: 50,000,000 shares; Issued: 11,911,057 cancelled September 16, 1987		11,911
Additional paid-in capital	2,262	19,922
Nonvested restricted stock awards	(399)	
Accumulated deficit		(115,745)
Retained earnings from September 17, 1987 (Note A)	(247)	
Total stockholders' equity (deficiency in assets)	2,223	(83,912)

7

Statements of Stockholders' Equity (Deficiency in Assets)
for the Years Ended December 31, 1985, 1986, and 1987
(in thousands)

	Common Stock Amount	Additional Paid-In Capital	Non-vested Restricted Stock Awards	Retained Earnings (Deficit)	Total
Balance December 31, 1986	$11,911	$ 19,922		$(115,745)	$(83,912)
Net income for the period ended September 16, 1987				264	264
Effect of confirmation of Plan and quasi-reorganization: (Note A)					
Cancellation of old common stock effective September 16, 1987	(11,911)				(11,911)
Issuance of nonvested stock options to executive management		418	(418)		
Settlement of prepetition liabilities under the Plan of Reorganization		77,048			77,048
Adjustment of debt issued pursuant to the Plan of Reorganization for imputation of interest at market rates		542			542
Key employee reorganization stock awards		(1,658)			(1,658)
Professional, legal and other expenses related to reorganization		(1,143)			(1,143)
Issuance of shares of new common stock to creditors, management and old common stock shareholders	440	16,781			17,221
Issuance of shares of common stock to investors in exchange for cash	167	5,833			6,000
Transfer of accumulated deficit to additional paid-in capital		(115,481)		115,481	
Balance September 17, 1987 (effective date of quasi-reorganization)	607	2,262	(418)		2,451
Net loss for the period September 17-December 31, 1987				(247)	(247)
Vesting of restricted stock awards			19		19
Balance December 31, 1987	$ 607	$ 2,262	$(399)	$ (247)	$ 2,223

See accompanying notes to financial statements.

Note A. Quasi-Reorganization

On September 23, 1985, the Company filed a petition for reorganization under Chapter 11 of the U.S. Bankruptcy Code in the United States Bankruptcy Court for the Southern District of New York (the "Bankruptcy Court"). In accordance with the provisions of the Bankruptcy Code, the Company continued operations as debtor-in-possession from September 23, 1985 to August 17, 1987.

On August 17, 1987, the Company's First Amended and Restated Plan of Reorganization (the "Plan") was confirmed by order of the Bankruptcy Court. In accordance with the Confirmation Order, the Company substantially consummated the Plan on September 17, 1987.

● ● ● ●

The Company accounted for the above as a quasi-reorganization. A quasi-reorganization is an elective, as opposed to mandatory, accounting procedure under Generally Accepted Accounting Principles intended to restate assets and liabilities to current fair market values, eliminate the deficit in retained earnings, and give the Company a "fresh start" from an accounting standpoint. The Company believes the discount on plan debt for the imputation of interest at market rates is the only significant adjustment to its assets and liabilities required to reflect fair value.

Note B. Significant Accounting Policies

● ● ● ●

Property and equipment. For periods prior to September 17, 1987, property and equipment are reported at values assigned upon assumption of ownership in January 1974, and at cost for assets acquired subsequent to that transaction. In conjunction with the quasi-reorganization on September 17, 1987, the book value of property and equipment was compared to fair market value and would have been adjusted had significant differences been identified. No such differences were identified. As a result, property and equipment are now stated at approximate fair market value at date of Plan consummation.

Depreciation is provided using the straight-line method over the estimated useful lives of three to ten years for equipment and machinery and fifteen to forty years for buildings, piers and ways. Amortization of the cost of leased equipment under capital leases is provided using the straight-line method over the respective lease terms and is included in depreciation and amortization expense. The remaining useful lives of all assets were reviewed at the date of Plan consummation, but no adjustment was considered necessary to reflect the remaining useful lives.

Accumulated depreciation as of September 16, 1987, was eliminated as part of the quasi-reorganization (Note A).

● ● ● ●

Note I. Debt

The Plan of Reorganization provides for the following long-term debt at December 31, 1987:

8-year mortgage note payable to former line bank creditors, bearing interest at the Federal Reserve Bank discount rate for years 1-2 and at the prime rate for years 3-8. Interest payments begin in the second year, with principal payments in years 3-8. Secured by a first lien on property, plant and equipment.	$6,500,000
Notes payable to taxing authorities in 6 equal annual cash payments bearing interest at 5-6%	2,296,000
	8,796,000
Less unamortized discount on plan debt to reflect current market value at the imputed rate of 8.75%; to be amortized using the interest method.	512,000
	8,284,000
Less current portion	305,000
	$7,979,000

● ● ● ●

THE VETA GRANDE COMPANIES, INC. AND SUBSIDIARIES

Consolidated Balance Sheets

	December 31	
	1987	1986
Shareholders' equity:		
Common stock, $0.01 par value; authorized 30,000,000 shares; issued and outstanding 16,983,569 shares in 1987 and 7,712,869 shares in 1986	169	77
Additional paid-in capital	16,828	8,511
Warrants outstanding	412	
Deficit	(8,587)	(365)
Total Shareholders' Equity	8,822	8,223

Consolidated Statements of Changes in Shareholders' Equity
for the Years Ended December 31, 1987, 1986, and 1985

	Common Stock Amount	Additional Paid-In Capital	Treasury Stock Amount	Deficit
Balance at January 1, 1985	$221	$41,400	$(1,962)	$(44,955)
Issuance of shares:				
Conversion of convertible notes and interest		5		
Settlement of debt and interest	26	591		
Remuneration for services rendered	9	53		
Contract settlement	3	31		
Legal settlement	25	225		
Retirement of old issue (Note 16)	(286)	(1,676)	1,962	
Issuance of new stock per plan of reorganization (Note 16):				
Common shareholders	14	(14)		
Preferred shareholders	19	931		
Convertible note holders		15		
Unsecured creditors	38	1,869		
Net income				10,040
Elimination of deficiency against additional paid-in capital in connection with reorganization (Note 16)		(34,915)		34,915
Balance at December 31, 1985	71	8,517		
Issuance of shares for additional claims of unsecured creditors in accordance with plan of reorganization (Note 16)	5	(5)		
Net loss				(365)
Balance at December 31, 1986	77	8,511		(365)
Issuance of shares:				
Remuneration for services	7	96		
Sale of shares	82	7,670		
Purchase of subsidiary	3	549		
Issuance of common stock warrants in remuneration for services				
Net loss				(8,056)
Common stock dividends ($.01 per share)				(166)
Balance at December 31, 1987	$169	$16,828		$ (8,587)

10

Notes to Consolidated Financial Statements

• • • •

16. Reorganization

On November 21, 1985, the Company filed a voluntary petition under Chapter 11 of the Federal Bankruptcy Code in the Central District of California, Case No. LA 85-17087-CA.

• • • •

The Federal Court approved claims for amounts in excess of those anticipated at December 31, 1985 by approximately $1,372,100 (including approximately $616,000 of claims discharged in the first quarter of 1987). These claims were discharged in accordance with the terms of the Plan and charged directly to additional paid-in capital as of December 31, 1986.

The Company accounted for the reorganization in a manner similar to a quasi-reorganization. It was determined that the historical book value of assets at December 31, 1985, in the aggregate, was substantially equivalent to fair value. The deficiency was eliminated against additional paid-in capital to reflect the new status of the Company as of December 31, 1985.

For financial purposes, the effects of this reorganization have been included in the financial statements of the Company as if the Plan of Reorganization were confirmed and claims were discharged on December 31, 1985. The deficit reflected in the financial statements represents the amount accumulated since December 31, 1985.

• • • •

VICTOR TECHNOLOGIES, INC. AND SUBSIDIARIES

Consolidated Balance Sheets
December 31, 1986 and 1985

	1986	1985
Shareholders' equity deficiency (Notes 2, 10 and 21):		
• • • •		
Common stock: $.01 par: authorized 20,000,000 shares; issued and outstanding 10,000,000 shares	100	100
Additional paid-in capital	17,895	17,895
Deficit subsequent to reorganization	(14,502)	(7,740)
	3,493	10,255

Consolidated Statements of Shareholders' Equity Deficiency
Years Ended December 31, 1986, 1985, and 1984

	Common Stock	Capital in Excess of Par	Retained Earnings (Deficit)
• • • •			
Balance, December 31, 1984	1,620	60,305	(109,535)
Loss from operations, January 1, 1985 to February 8, 1985 (Note 19)			(914)
Forgiveness of indebtedness (Note 8)			57,458
Impact of reorganization, February 8, 1985	(1,610)	(51,381)	52,991
Sale of stock, February 8, 1985	90	8,971	
Balance, February 8, 1985	100	17,895	
Loss from operations, February 9, 1985 to December 31, 1985 (Note 19)			(7,740)
Balance, December 31, 1985	100	17,895	(7,740)
Net loss for 1986			(6,762)
Balance, December 31, 1986	$ 100	$17,895	($14,502)

• • • •

2. Plan of reorganization

On February 6, 1984, the Company, excluding its European subsidiaries, filed a voluntary petition for reorganization under Chapter 11 of the United States Bankruptcy Code (following an involuntary filing against one of the Company's subsidiaries on February 3, 1984).

• • • •

The balance sheets represent the Company's consolidated financial position at December 31, 1986 and 1985, the Company's fiscal year-end. The financial statements subsequent to February 8, 1985, are presented under quasi-reorganization provisions in accordance with which the deficit at the reorganization date is offset against available additional paid-in capital. The carrying value of the assets is continued at the recorded value as this approximates the assets' fair value.

III

ASSETS NOT RESTATED—DID NOT STATE THAT RESTATEMENT IS UNNECESSARY

As discussed in chapter 2, some companies that have applied quasi-reorganizations and have not restated assets said that restatement was unnecessary because the fair values of assets equalled the carrying values. Other companies that applied quasi-reorganizations without restating assets did not say that restatement was unnecessary. Twenty-two examples of such companies are presented below. The examples are classified according to whether the company was or was not being reorganized in bankruptcy at the time of the quasi-reorganization.

NOT UNDER BANKRUPTCY PROCEEDING

AMERICAN BARRICK RESOURCES CORPORATION

Consolidated Balance Sheets
as at December 31, 1986 and 1985
(in thousands)

	1986	1985
Shareholders' equity:		
Capital stock (note 12)	127,790	134,385
Retained earnings (deficit)	13,617	(47,370)
	141,407	87,015

Consolidated Statements of Retained Earnings
for the Years Ended December 31, 1986, 1985, 1984
(in thousands)

	1986
Deficit at beginning of year	$(47,370)
Elimination of deficit by reduction in stated capital (note 12)	47,370
Net income (loss) for the year	15,062
Costs incurred in raising capital (net of income taxes of $1,500)	(1,445)

• • • •

Retained earnings (deficit) at end of year	$ 13,617

Notes to Consolidated Financial Statements
(tabular dollar amounts in thousands)

● ● ● ●

12. Capital Stock

● ● ● ●

On May 28, 1986, the shareholders of the Company approved a reduction in the stated capital of the common shares of $47,370,000, which eliminated the deficit as at December 31, 1985.

● ● ● ●

CAMPBELL RESOURCES INC.

Consolidated Balance Sheet
(in thousands of Canadian dollars)

	As at December 31, 1986	As at June 30 1986	As at June 30 1985
Shareholders' Equity			
Capital Stock (Note 10)	112,602	104,296	168,641
Currency Translation Adjustments	978	1,009	2,288
Deficit (December 31, 1986 and June 30, 1986—from July 1, 1985)	(15,168)	(16,043)	(95,678)
	98,412	89,262	75,251

Consolidated Statement of Retained Earnings (Deficit)
(in thousands of Canadian dollars)

	For the Six Months Ended December 31, 1986	For the Year Ended June 30 1986	For the Year Ended June 30 1985	For the Year Ended June 30 1984
Balance (deficit) at beginning of the period	$(16,043)	$ (95,678)	$ 14,065	$ 32,712
Net income (loss)	875	(16,043)	(108,272)	(12,774)
	(15,168)	(111,721)	(94,207)	19,938
Stock dividend on common shares				(2,683)
Dividends on preference shares			(1,471)	(3,190)
Reduction in stated capital (Note 10)		95,678		
Balance (deficit) at end of the period	$(15,168)	$ (16,043)	$ (95,678)	$ 14,065

Notes to the Consolidated Financial Statements
December 31, 1986

● ● ● ●

10. Capital Stock

● ● ● ●

b. *Common shares.*

(i) Changes in the issued and outstanding common shares during the six months ended December 31, 1986, and each of the three years ended June 30, 1986, were as follows:

(in thousands)	Six Months Ended December 31, 1986 Ascribed Value	Year Ended June 30 1986 Ascribed Value
Balance at beginning of the period	• • • •	$126,965
	• • • •	
Issued on conversions, exercise of warrants and under employee incentive plan		74
Issued on exchange of preference shares and debentures		64,153
Reduction of stated capital to eliminate the consolidated deficit at June 30, 1985		(95,678)
Dissenting shareholders' redemption		(495)
Issued for payment of interest on convertible debentures		1,440
	• • • •	
Issued in connection with 1985 exploration program		4,380
Issued in connection with 1986 exploration program		3,980
	• • • •	
Contingency payments on prior years' acquisitions		(523)
Balance at end of the period		$104,296

• • • •

(ii) Information concerning common shares:

The shareholders approved, at a special meeting held on September 11, 1985, a capital reorganization of Campbell which resulted in the exchange of all the issued and outstanding preference shares for common shares and warrants, the exchange of all the issued and outstanding convertible debentures for common shares and warrants and the reduction of Campbell's stated capital by an amount that eliminated the consolidated deficit at June 30, 1985.

• • • •

CERTRON CORPORATION AND SUBSIDIARY

Consolidated Balance Sheets

	October 31	
	1983	1982
STOCKHOLDERS' EQUITY (Notes 2 and 4):		
Common stock, no par value; stated value $1 per share; authorized 10,000,000 shares	3,041	2,911
Additional paid-in capital	1,549	1,324
Retained earnings since August 1, 1982	623	252
	5,213	4,487

Consolidated Statements of Stockholders' Equity

	Common Stock Amount	Additional Paid-In Capital	Retained Earnings (Deficit)	Treasury Stock Amount
BALANCE, November 1, 1980	$2,921	$ 9,638	$(10,252)	$(9)
Net earnings				
Exercise of stock options	2	(1)		
Preferred dividends			(57)	
Redemption of preferred stock and warrants		639		
BALANCE, October 31, 1981	2,923	10,276	(9,563)	(9)
Retirement of treasury shares	(12)	3		9
Preferred dividends				
Redemption of preferred stock and warrants				
Net earnings for the nine months ended July 31, 1982			127	
Elimination of retained earnings deficit through a corporate equity adjustment as of August 1, 1982		(9,443)	9,443	
Net earnings for the three months ended October 31, 1982			252	
Increase in paid-in capital resulting from the carryforward of prior years' net operating losses		201		
BALANCE, October 31, 1982	2,911	1,324	252	
Exercise of stock options	130	(16)		
Tax benefit related to stock options		53		
Net earnings for the twelve months ended October 31, 1983			371	
Increase in paid-in capital resulting from the carryforward of prior years' net operating losses		188		
BALANCE, October 31, 1983	$3,041	$ 1,549	$ 623	

See notes to consolidated financial statements.

Notes to Consolidated Financial Statements
Years Ended October 31, 1983, 1982, and 1981

• • • •

Note 2. Corporate Equity Adjustment

As a result of the final redemption of preferred stock in the third quarter of 1982 (Note 4), the Company's Board of Directors approved a Corporate Equity Adjustment effective August 1, 1982, in which the $9,443,000 deficit accumulated through that date was eliminated against additional paid-in capital. Retained earnings at October 31, 1983, represent the consolidated earnings of the Company and its subsidiary subsequent to August 1, 1982.

• • • •

COMPUCOM SYSTEMS, INC.

Balance Sheets

	December 31	
	1987	1986
Shareholders' Equity (Deficit)		
Preferred stock, stated value $.001 a share; Authorized 10,000,000 shares; Outstanding 1987—none, 1986 1,227,800 shares		1
Common stock, stated value $.001 a share Authorized 30,000,000 shares Issued 1987—23,050,534 shares; 1986—10,922,876 shares	23	11
Additional paid-in capital	8,754	16,590
Accumulated deficit		(22,001)
Retained earnings from July 1, 1987	877	
Treasury stock....	(43)	
Total shareholders' equity (deficit)	9,611	(5,399)

Statements of Shareholders' Equity (Deficit)

	Preferred Stock	Common Stock Amount	Additional Paid-In Capital	Accumulated Deficit	Retained Earnings	Treasury Stock
Balance— December 31, 1984		$ 7	$ 5,599	$ (4,180)		
• • • •						
Balance— December 31, 1986	1	11	16,590	(22,001)		
Issuance of common stock and warrants		9	11,651			
Exercise of warrants		2	3,021			
Exercise of options			161			
Conversion of preferred stock	(1)	1				
Purchase of treasury stock						$(43)
Net loss— January 1 to June 30				(1,278)		
Deficit reclassification			(23,279)	23,279		
Net earnings— July 1 to December 31					$1,487	
Tax benefit related to deficit reclassification			610		(610)	
Balance— December 31, 1987		$23	$ 8,754		$ 877	$(43)

See notes to financial statements and summary of accounting policies.

Summary of Accounting Policies

• • • •

Restructuring. In connection with the TriStar acquisition and the discontinued machine vision operations, the Company reclassified its accumulated deficit as of July 1, 1987, as a reduction of additional paid-in-capital to better reflect the financial position and new operating focus of the Company. Retained earnings as of December 31, 1987, represents the net earnings of the Company since July 1, 1987.

Prior year amounts have been reclassified to reflect the discontinued vision operations and to conform to the 1987 presentation.

• • • •

CONQUEST EXPLORATION COMPANY

Consolidated Balance Sheets
(in thousands)

	December 31, 1986	Restated December 31, 1985
Shareholders' Equity		
Preferred stock, $1.00 par value, 25,000,000 shares authorized, 5,000,000 shares issued and outstanding at December 31, 1986, aggregate liquidating preference of $23,750	5,000	
Common stock, $.20 par value, 75,000,000 shares authorized	5,966	4,326
Paid-in capital	74,096	69,721
Treasury stock, at cost	(230)	(230)
Retained earnings (deficit):		
Prior to January 1, 1986 (eliminated in quasi-reorganization effective January 1, 1986)		(47,356)
Since January 1, 1986	(10,301)	
	74,531	26,461

Consolidated Statements of Shareholders' Equity
(in thousands)

	Common Stock Amount	Preferred Stock Amount	Paid-In Capital	Retained Earnings	Treasury Stock
	• • • •				
Balance at December 31, 1985	4,326		69,721	(47,356)	
Quasi-Reorganization			(47,356)	47,356	(230)
Issuances of stock					
Public offering of units	640		12,752		
Sale to The Dyson-Kissner-Moran Corporation	1,000	5,000	38,964		
Exercise of stock options			15		
Exercise of warrants					
Dividends on preferred stock				(495)	
Net loss				(9,806)	
Balance at December 31, 1986	$5,966	$5,000	$74,096	$(10,301)	$(230)

Notes to Consolidated Financial Statements

1. Organization and Summary of Significant Accounting Policies
   Organization.

● ● ● ●

    The Company's Board of Directors approved a quasi-reorganization effective January 1, 1986 in which the retained earnings deficit at December 31, 1985, of $47,356,000 was eliminated against paid-in capital. Total shareholders' equity is unchanged. The retained earnings deficit at December 31, 1986, includes the losses of the Company subsequent to the effective date of the quasi-reorganization.

● ● ● ●

FMI FINANCIAL CORPORATION

Consolidated Balance Sheet
(in thousands)

	December 31, 1983	January 31, 1983
STOCKHOLDERS' EQUITY (Note 5):		
Preferred Stock, including additional paid-in capital	39,645	44,356
Common Stock, $.01 par, including additional paid-in capital (100 million shares authorized, 12,973,336 and 9,822,474 shares issued and outstanding)	76,758	145,372
Retained earnings (deficit)		(102,850)
Net unrealized gain on marketable equity securities	75	
	116,478	86,878

Consolidated Statement of Changes in Stockholders' Equity
(in thousands)

	Eleven Months Ended December 31, 1983
Preferred Stock Class A and Additional Paid-In Capital:	
Balance at beginning of period	$ 211
Conversion of shares	(60)
Redemption of shares	(151)

● ● ● ●

Balance at end of period	
Preferred Stock Class B and Additional Paid-In Capital:	
Balance at beginning of period	44,145
Conversion of shares	(4,500)
Balance at end of period	39,645
Common Stock and Additional Paid-In Capital:	
Balance at beginning of period	145,372
Conversion of Class A and B Preferred Stock	4,560
Exercise of warrants	2,260
Redemption of warrants	(450)
Issuance of warrants with senior subordinated Notes	18,150

● ● ● ●

Consolidated Statement of Changes in Stockholders' Equity (continued)
(in thousands)

	Eleven Months Ended December 31, 1983
Other	(7)
Transfer of accumulated deficit as of December 31, 1983 to additional paid-in capital	(93,127)
Balance at end of period	76,758
Retained Earnings (Deficit):	
Balance at beginning of period	(102,850)
Net Income (loss) for period	9,723
Transfer of accumulated deficit as of December 31, 1983 to additional paid-in capital	93,127
Balance at end of period	
Net Unrealized Gain on Marketable Equity Securities:	
Balance at beginning of period	
Change during period	75
Balance at end of period	75

Notes to Consolidated Financial Statements

• • • •

5. Stockholders' Equity.

• • • •

As of December 31, 1983, $93.1 million of additional paid-in capital attributable to Common Stock was applied to eliminate the accumulated deficit at that date. As a consequence, subsequent to December 31, 1983, undistributed net income will be reflected as retained earnings and the tax benefit of the utilization of the net operating loss carryforward will be reflected in additional paid-in capital attributable to Common Stock.

• • • •

GENENTECH, INC.

Consolidated Balance Sheet
(in thousands)

	December 31	
	1987	1986
Stockholders' equity:		
• • • •		
Common Stock, $.02 par value; authorized 297,000,000 shares; outstanding: 1987—78,739,896 shares; 1986—76,949,500 shares	1,575	1,539
Earnings Convertible Restricted Stock, $.02 par value; authorized 3,000,000 shares; outstanding 1987 and 1986: 2,927,260 shares	59	59
Additional paid-in capital	336,267	635,883
Notes receivable from sale of stock	(320)	(351)
Accumulated deficit		(344,514)
Retained earnings (since October 1, 1987 quasi-reorganization in which a deficit of $329,457 was eliminated)	17,831	
Total stockholders' equity	355,412	292,616

Consolidated Statements of Stockholders' Equity
(in thousands)

	Common Stock	Restricted Stock	Additional Paid-In Capital	Notes Receivable From Sale of Stock	Retained Earnings (Accumulated Deficit)
Balance at December 31, 1986	1,539	59	635,883	(351)	(344,514)
Issuance of Common Stock—(1,489,839 shares)	30		16,915		
Payments on notes receivable				29	
Net income January 1 through September 30, 1987					15,057
Balance at September 30, 1987, before quasi-reorganization	1,569	59	652,798	(322)	(329,457)
Quasi-Reorganization			(329,457)		329,457
Balance at October 1, 1987, after quasi-reorganization	1,569	59	323,341	(322)	
Issuance of Common Stock—(300,557 shares)	6		3,584		
Payments on notes receivable				2	
Net income October 1 through December 31, 1987					27,173
Tax benefits arising prior to quasi-reorganization			9,342		(9,342)
Balance at December 31, 1987	$1,575	$59	$336,267	$(320)	$ 17,831

See notes to consolidated financial statements.

Notes to Consolidated Financial Statements

• • • •

Note 6. Quasi-Reorganization

On February 18, 1988, the Company's Board of Directors approved the elimination of the Company's accumulated deficit through an accounting reorganization of its stockholders' equity accounts (a quasi-reorganization) effective October 1, 1987. The quasi-reorganization did not involve any revaluation of assets or liabilities. The effective date of the quasi-reorganization (October 1, 1987) reflects the beginning of the quarter in which Genentech received approval for and commenced marketing of its second major product, and as such, marks a turning point in the Company's operations. The accumulated deficit was eliminated by a transfer from additional paid-in capital in an amount equal to the accumulated deficit. The Company's stockholders' equity accounts at October 1, 1987, before and after the quasi-reorganization, are reflected in the consolidated statements of stockholders' equity. The tax benefits related to items occurring prior to the quasi-reorganization have been reclassified from retained earnings to additional paid-in capital.

• • • •

KAISER STEEL CORPORATION

Consolidated Balance Sheet
(in thousands)

	December 31, 1983
Shareholders' Equity:	
Series A preferred stock	50,478
Series B preferred stock	7,478
Common stock	1,000
Capital surplus (Note P)	89,739

Consolidated Statement of Stockholders' Equity
(in thousands)

	Series B Preferred Stock	$1.46 Preferred Stock	Common Stock	Capital Surplus	Retained Earnings (Deficit)
Balance, January 1, 1983		$9,337	$4,845	$ 84,451	$166,486
Net loss					(422,770)
Cash dividend on preferred stock—$1.46 per share					(514)
Purchase and retirement of preferred stock	(1,000)			17	
To record purchase accounting adjustments (Note C):					
Purchase and retirement of preferred stock		(8,337)		71	
Payment of $22 per share of common stock			(4,845)		(156,591)
Issuance of 10,000,000 shares of common stock, 10 cents par value			1,000		
Gain on defeasance of Pollution Control Revenue Bonds				7,464	
Payment for option on 1,181,100 shares of common stock, 66⅔ cents par value				(14,532)	
Allocation of purchase price:					
Net tangible assets				384,949	
Excess of purchase price over fair value of net assets acquired				98,664	
Less: Par value of Series B preferred stock	7,478			(7,478)	
Assigned value of Series A preferred stock				(50,478)	
Capitalization of deficit (Note P)				(413,389)	413,389
Balance, December 31, 1983	$7,478	$ 0	$1,000	$ 89,739	$ 0

See notes to consolidated financial statements.

Notes to Consolidated Financial Statements

• • • •

Note P. Capitalization of Deficit

As of December 31, 1983, the Company has charged the accumulated deficit to capital surplus. Accordingly, retained earnings will represent only the results of operations for periods subsequent to December 31, 1983.

• • • •

L.D. BRINKMAN CORPORATION AND SUBSIDIARIES

Consolidated Balance Sheets
(in thousands)

	July 31		
	1983	1982	1981
Stockholders' Equity:			
Preferred stock—3,000 shares in 1983 and 1982 and 2,000 shares in 1981 stated at par value	3	3	2
Common stock—$1 par value, authorized 15,000,000 shares, issued 6,460,107 in 1983, 4,670,107 in 1982 and 3,670,107 in 1981	6,460	4,670	3,670
Paid-in capital	37,877	23,761	44,620
Retained earnings (Deficit):			
From August 1, 1981	11,107	4,237	
Deficit transferred to paid-in capital on August 1, 1981			(26,876)
Treasury stock—common, at cost....	(1,307)	(1,350)	(1,358)
Total stockholders' equity	54,140	31,321	20,058

Consolidated Statement of Stockholders' Equity
for the three years ended July 31, 1983
(in thousands)

	Non-Redeemable Preferred Stock	Common Stock	Paid-In Capital	Retained Earnings (Deficit)	Treasury Stock
Balance at July 31, 1981	$2	$3,670	$ 44,620	$(26,876)	$(1,358)
Transfer of deficit			(26,876)	26,876	
Treasury stock issued in connection with stock options exercised (3,400 shares)			(5)		8
Preferred dividends declared				(825)	
Common stock issued (1,000,000 shares) in exchange for $1,000,000 liquidation of Series I Preferred Stock		1,000			
Issuance of 1,000 shares of Series L Preferred Stock $1.00 par value	1		4,599		
Increase in paid-in capital resulting from the liquidation of the Series I Preferred Stock and the issuance of the Series L Preferred Stock			1,423		
Net income				5,062	
Balance at July 31, 1982	3	4,670	23,761	4,237	(1,350)
Preferred dividends declared				(713)	

Consolidated Statement of Stockholders' Equity (continued)
for the three years ended July 31, 1983
(in thousands)

	Non-Redeemable Preferred Stock	Common Stock	Paid-In Capital	Retained Earnings (Deficit)	Treasury Stock
Treasury stock issued in connection with stock options exercised (26,400 shares)			66		43
Shares issued upon exercise of officer's stock option		150	469		
Shares issued upon exercise of $1.50 warrants		500	250		
Sale of common stock net of registration expenses of $292,000 (1,140,000 shares)		1,140	13,331		
Net income				7,583	
Balance at July 31, 1983	$3	$6,460	$ 37,877	$ 11,107	$(1,307)

Notes to Consolidated Financial Statements

• • • •

Note 7. Adjustment to Stockholders' Equity

The Board of Directors of the Company approved at a meeting held on October 18, 1982, an adjustment in the Company's Stockholders' Equity accounts to eliminate the Deficit effective August 1, 1981, by charging $26,876,000 against Paid-In Capital.

The greatest portion of the Deficit ($45,615,000 at July 31, 1977) was incurred by the Company prior to July 31, 1977 and relates primarily to operations that did not exist at that date. During the period from August 1, 1977 through July 31, 1981, operations of the Company have resulted in net earnings of $18,739,000.

• • • •

THE LVI GROUP, INC. AND SUBSIDIARIES

Consolidated Balance Sheet
December 31

	1986	1985
	(in thousands)	
Shareholders' equity:		
• • • •		
Common stock, par value $.50 per share; authorized 30,000,000 shares, issued 20,181,000 and 18,927,000 shares of which 138,855 shares are held as treasury stock	10,091	9,464
Additional paid-in capital	7,984	39,999
Accumulated deficit		(35,997)
Retained earnings from January 1, 1986	2,948	
Foreign currency translation adjustment	14	
Less treasury stock—at cost	(493)	(493)
Total shareholders' equity	20,544	12,973

24

Consolidated Statement of Changes in Shareholders' Equity
Years Ended December 31, 1986, 1985, and 1984
(in thousands)

	Non-Redeemable Preferred Stock	Common Stock	Additional Paid-In Capital	Accumulated Deficit	Retained Earnings From January 1 1986	Treasury Stock
Balance, January 1, 1984	$3,342	$ 4,029	$21,203	$(25,626)		$(493)
Acquisition of 28,000 shares of redeemable preferred stock			450			
Net loss—1984				(2,196)		
Balance, December 31, 1984	3,342	4,029	21,653	(27,822)		(493)
Exercise of stock warrants		50	137			
Conversion of preferred stock and dividends	(3,342)	1,608	5,850	(3,556)		
Issuance of common stock in connection with NICO, Inc. acquisition		3,701	12,030			
Issuance of common stock in connection with Smith-Thibault Corporation acquisition		76	329			
Net loss—1985				(4,619)		
Balance, December 31, 1985		9,464	39,999	(35,997)		(493)
Quasi-reorganization			(35,997)	35,997		
Increase in foreign currency translation adjustment						
Issuance of common stock in connection with HRF Environmental Services, Inc. acquisition		195	997			
Issuance of common stock in exchange for subordinated debentures		352	2,908			
Issuance of common stock from options exercised		80	77			
Net income—1986					$2,948	
Balance, December 31, 1986		$10,091	$ 7,984		$2,948	(493)

Notes to Consolidated Financial Statements
(Tables included in the footnotes are in thousands except for per share data)

1. Organization

• • • •

On March 25, 1986, the Company's Board of Directors approved a readjustment of accounts effected in the form of a "quasi-reorganization." Effective January 1, 1986, the balance in accumulated deficit was transferred to additional paid-in capital and accordingly retained earnings is dated effective January 1, 1986.

• • • •

THE MERCHANT BANK OF CALIFORNIA AND SUBSIDIARY

Consolidated Balance Sheets
December 31, 1986 and 1985

	1986	1985
Stockholders' Equity (Notes 8 and 9):		
• • • •		
Common stock, no par value—authorized 9,000,000 shares; issued and outstanding 5,431,102 shares in 1986 and 721,302 shares in 1985	4,352	2,885
Surplus		2,866
Undivided profits (deficit) after writing off $5,747,798 to surplus and common stock as of July 31, 1986	(2,709)	(5,348)
Total stockholders' equity	1,642	403

Consolidated Statements of Changes in Stockholders' Equity
for the Years Ended December 31, 1986, 1985, and 1984

	Common Stock	Surplus	Undivided Profits (Deficit)	Total
Balance, December 31, 1983	$2,885	$2,866	$ (723)	$5,028
Net income for the year			507	507
Balance, December 31, 1984	2,885	2,866	(215)	5,536
Net loss for the year			(5,133)	(5,133)
Balance, December 31, 1985	2,885	2,866	(5,348)	403
Sale of common stock, net (Note 8)	4,348			4,348
Net loss for the year			(3,108)	(3,108)
Write-off of the deficit in undivided profits against surplus and common stock (Note 8)	(2,881)	(2,866)	5,747	
Balance, December 31, 1986	$4,352		$(2,709)	$1,642

The accompanying notes are an integral part of these consolidated statements.

Notes to Consolidated Financial Statements
December 31, 1986

1. Regulatory Requirements

As a result of an examination conducted by the Federal Deposit Insurance Corporation (FDIC), on March 7, 1986, The Merchant Bank of California and Subsidiary (the Bank) consented to an Order to

Cease and Desist which required, among other things, that the Bank take the steps necessary to increase total equity capital and reserves by $3,500,000, or whatever greater amount was needed to raise its adjusted equity capital and reserves to equal or exceed 6.5 percent of average adjusted total assets for the month of March, 1986, provide management acceptable to the FDIC and provide a plan to reduce the Bank's use of brokered deposits. The Order further required that the Bank have adjusted equity capital and reserves to equal or exceed 7.5 percent of average adjusted total assets for the month of March 1987 and thereafter. On March 7, 1986, the Bank consented to an Order from the California State Banking Department (SBD) with requirements similar to those contained in the FDIC's Order.

On November 7, 1985, the SBD informed the Bank that its capital was impaired by $2,493,000 at September 30, 1985. On February 11, 1986, the SBD issued an amended Order requiring the Bank to correct its capital impairment of $3,048,000 existing as of December 31, 1985. The SBD considers a bank's capital to be impaired when the deficit in undivided profits exceeds 40 percent of contributed capital. As more fully described in Note 8, the Bank raised $4,348,000 in additional equity capital through the sale of common stock. On July 31, 1986, the Bank effected an elimination of the deficit in undivided profits against contributed capital through a procedure allowed under state banking law with the approval of the SBD and the Bank's stockholders, thereby curing its capital impairment.

• • • •

8. Stockholders' Equity

• • • •

On July 31, 1986, the Bank effected an elimination of the deficit in undivided profits against contributed capital through a procedure allowed under state banking law with the approval of the State Banking Department and the Bank's stockholders.

• • • •

MISSISSIPPI CHEMICAL CORPORATION AND SUBSIDIARIES

Consolidated Balance Sheets
(in thousands)

	June 30	
	1988	1987
Shareholder-Members' Equity (Notes 3, 4 and 12):		
Common stock:		
Nitrogen series	25,754	25,754
Mixed series	16,593	16,593
Potash series	213	213
Additional paid-in capital	54,046	66,168
Capital equity credits	42,913	32,301
Accumulated deficit prior to June 30, 1988		(19,619)
Retained earnings beginning June 30, 1988		
	139,519	121,410

Consolidated Statements of Shareholder-Members' Equity
(in thousands)

	Common Stock			Additional Paid-In Capital	Capital Equity Credits	Retained Earnings (Deficit)
	Nitrogen Series	Mixed Series	Potash Series			
Balances, July 1, 1985	$25,754	$16,593	$213	$65,999	$37,070	$20,523
Revolved capital equity credits					(4,016)	
Capital equity credits cancelled				169	(369)	
Net loss						(12,780)

Consolidated Statements of Shareholder-Members' Equity (continued)
(in thousands)

	Common Stock			Additional Paid-In Capital	Capital Equity Credits	Retained Earnings (Deficit)
	Nitrogen Series	Mixed Series	Potash Series			
Balances, June 30, 1986	25,754	16,593	213	66,168	32,685	7,743
Capital equity credits cancelled					(384)	
Net loss						(27,362)
Balances, June 30, 1987	25,754	16,593	213	66,168	32,301	(19,619)
Capital equity credits cancelled					(5)	
Capital equity credits issued as patronage refunds					10,617	
Transfer of deficit to paid-in capital due to quasi-reorganization as of June 30, 1988 (Note 12)				(12,122)		12,122
Net earnings						7,497
Balances, June 30, 1988	$25,754	$16,593	$213	$54,046	$42,913	$ 0

See summary of significant accounting policies and notes
to consolidated financial statements.

Notes to Consolidated Financial Statements
Years Ended June 30, 1988, 1987, and 1986

• • • •

Note 12. Quasi-Reorganization

A majority of the Company's shareholders voting at a special shareholders' meeting on August 23, 1988, approved a plan of quasi-reorganization effective as of June 30, 1988. In accordance with the approved plan, the Company's accumulated deficit of $12,122,000 was transferred to additional paid-in capital. This transaction has been reflected in the Company's financial statements as of June 30, 1988.

• • • •

PUBLIC SERVICE COMPANY OF INDIANA, INC.

Balance Sheets

	December 31	
	1986	1985
	(thousands)	
Common Stock Equity (Notes 5 and 6):		
Common stock—without par value; $.01 stated value 1986 —authorized 60,000,000 shares—outstanding 53,854,554 shares	$ 539	$1,066,042
Paid-in capital	140,095	
Accumulated deficit		(893,794)
Accumulated earnings subsequent to November 30, 1986 quasi-reorganization, in which a deficit of $925,408 was eliminated	9,536	
Total common stock equity	150,170	172,248

Statements of Changes in Common Stock Equity

	Common Stock	Paid-In Capital	Accumulated Earnings (Deficit)
		(thousands)	
Balance December 31, 1983	$1,065,492		$ 404,596
Net income for 1984			85,518
Common stock issued (45,441 shares)	550		
Cash dividends			
Preferred stock			(28,540)
Common stock			(53,855)
Balance December 31, 1984	1,066,042		407,719
Net income (loss) for 1985			(1,219,118)
Cash dividends			
Preferred stock			(28,540)
Common stock			(53,855)
Balance December 31, 1985	1,066,042		(893,794)
Net income (loss) for January through November 1986			(31,614)
Balance November 30, 1986 before quasi-reorganization	1,066,042		(925,408)
Quasi-Reorganization (Note 5)	(1,065,503)	140,095	925,408
Balance November 30, 1986 after quasi-reorganization	539	140,095	
Net income for December 1986			9,536
Balance December 31, 1986	$ 539	$140,095	$ 9,536

Notes to Financial Statements

• • • •

5. Quasi-Reorganization

On December 10, 1986, the Board approved the elimination of the Company's accumulated deficit through an accounting reorganization of its common stock equity accounts (a quasi-reorganization) effective November 30, 1986. To consummate the quasi-reorganization, the Board assigned a stated value of $.01 per share to the Company's common stock, resulting in a restated balance of $.5 million. The difference between the common stock balance before restatement of $1,066 million and the restated balance of $.5 million was transferred to paid-in capital. Concurrently, the accumulated deficit was eliminated by a transfer from paid-in capital in an amount equal to the accumulated deficit. The Company's common stock equity accounts at November 30, 1986, before and after the quasi-reorganization, are reflected in the Statements of Changes in Common Stock Equity.

• • • •

TRITON ENERGY CORPORATION AND SUBSIDIARIES

Consolidated Balance Sheets
May 31, 1986 and 1985

	1986	1985
Stockholders' equity (Notes 6, 8 and 9):		
$11 convertible, exchangeable preferred stock, no par value; authorized 5,000,000 shares; issued and outstanding 243,000 shares		22,146
$2 convertible, exchangeable preferred stock, no par value; authorized 5,000,000 shares; issued and outstanding 2,300,000 shares	54,905	

Consolidated Balance Sheets (continued)
May 31, 1986 and 1985

	1986	1985
Common stock, par value $1; authorized 25,000,000 shares; issued 8,970,531 shares in 1986 and 7,378,995 shares in 1985	8,971	7,379
Additional paid-in capital	52,625	56,247
Retained earnings, reflecting a corporate readjustment of $28,653,000 in 1986 (Note 8)		21,148
Valuation reserve on noncurrent marketable securities	(4,070)	
Foreign currency translation adjustment	(8,115)	(9,832)
	104,316	97,088
Less cost of common stock in treasury	23	221
Total stockholders' equity	104,293	96,867

Consolidated Statements of Stockholders' Equity
Three Years Ended May 31, 1986

	Preferred Stock	Common Stock	Additional Paid-In Capital	Retained Earnings	Treasury Stock	Total Stockholders' Equity
Balance at May 31, 1985	$22,146	$7,379	$56,247	$21,148	$221	$ 96,867
Net loss				(42,387)		(42,387)
Cash dividends, $.10 per common share				(857)		(857)
Cash dividends, $.3836 per $2 preferred share				(882)		(882)
Cash dividends, $5.50 per $11 preferred share				(1,337)		(1,337)
3% stock dividend		220	4,092	(4,338)		(26)
Conversion of 243,000 shares of $11 preferred stock, net of issue costs	(22,146)	1,339	20,554			(253)
Issuance of $2 preferred stock net of issue costs, 2,300,000 shares	54,905					54,905
Treasury stock acquired					(1)	1
Stock options exercised		13	26		(197)	236
Shares issued in connection with conversion of 10% convertible debt		20	359			379
Foreign currency translation adjustment						1,717

	Preferred Stock	Common Stock	Additional Paid-In Capital	Retained Earnings	Treasury Stock	Total Stock-holders' Equity
Unrealized loss on noncurrent marketable securities						(4,070)
Corporate re-adjustment (Note 8)			(28,653)	28,653		
Balance at May 31, 1986	$54,905	$8,971	$52,625	$ 0	$ 23	$104,293

Notes to Consolidated Financial Statements
Three Years Ended May 31, 1986

• • • •

8. Stockholders' Equity

• • • •

In order to permit the Company to pay common stock dividends from future earnings without being penalized by an accumulated deficit, Article 4.13B of the Texas Business Corporation Act provides that a Company may, subject to its Board of Directors approval, eliminate that deficit through application of additional paid-in capital. Pursuant to Board of Directors approval on August 6, 1986, the Company eliminated its accumulated deficit of $28,653,000 at May 31, 1986.

UNDER BANKRUPTCY PROCEEDING

COLONIAL COMMERCIAL CORP. AND SUBSIDIARIES

Consolidated Balance Sheets
December 31, 1983 and 1982

	1983	1982
Stockholders' equity:		
Convertible preferred stock (par value $.01. Authorized 12,444,300 shares; issued and outstanding 12,083,378 in 1983 and 12,444,300 shares to be issued in 1982)	120	124
Additional paid-in capital	9,052	7,259
Retained earnings since January 1, 1983	715	
Preferred stockholders' equity (liquidation and redemption value $12,083,378 in 1983 and $12,444,300 in 1982)	9,889	7,384
Common stock par value $.01. Authorized 19,300,000 shares; issued and outstanding 3,419,104 in 1983 and 3,055,641 in 1982	34	30
	9,923	7,414

Consolidated Statements of Stockholders' Equity (Deficit)
Years Ended December 31, 1983, 1982, and 1981

	Convertible Preferred Stock	Additional Paid-In Capital	Common Stock	Retained Earnings (Deficit)	Treasury Stock	Total Stock-holders' Equity (Deficit)
Balance at December 31, 1981		$ 4,705	$1,546	$(14,539)	$(89)	$ (8,377)
Net (loss)				(2,556)		(2,556)
Effect of confirmation of plan and quasi-reorganization:						
Change in par value of common stock from $.50 per share to $.01 per share		1,515	(1,515)			
Net gain on the settlement of liabilities		10,964				10,964
Convertible preferred stock to be issued	$124	7,259				7,384
Retirement of treasury stock		(89)			89	
Deficit charged to additional Paid-in capital		(17,095)		17,095		
Balance at December 31, 1982	124	7,259	30			7,414
Net income				715		715
Gain on reorganization of Big Smith, Inc.		1,522				1,522
Gain on reorganization of Colonial		253				253
Conversion of convertible preferred stock	(3)		3			
Issuance of common stock	—	16				17
Balance at December 31, 1983	$120	$ 9,052	$ 34	$ 715	$ 0	$ 9,923

Notes to Consolidated Financial Statements
December 31, 1983

• • • •

2. Colonial Chapter 11 Proceedings and Quasi-Reorganization

The Company, which had been operating under the supervision of the U.S. Bankruptcy Court since November 30, 1981, had its sixth amended Plan of Reorganization (the Plan) confirmed by the Court on January 5, 1983, and recorded the transaction as of December 31, 1982. Under the Plan the Company

32

issued 12,475,358 shares of convertible preferred stock, 3,179,033 Class A Warrants and $2,946,099 principal amount of 6% notes (including 60,449 shares of convertible preferred stock, 15,167 Class A Warrants and $14,335 principal amount of 6% notes held by a subsidiary of the Company). In addition to the issuance of new securities, the Plan provided for increasing the Company's authorized common stock to 19,300,000 shares and reducing the par value of such stock from $.50 to $.01 per share. The Plan also provided for cash payment in full for priority creditors and Plan administrative expenses. The recording of the settlements under the Plan resulted in a gain of $10,964,365 in 1982 as follows:

Elimination of liabilities deferred	$22,675,780
Issuance of 6% notes....	(3,706,620)
Issuance of convertible preferred stock....	(7,384,399)
Payments to priority creditors	(90,698)
Expenses of settlement plan	(529,698)
Net gain	$10,964,365

• • • •

Simultaneously upon emergence from Chapter 11 proceedings, the Company effected a "Quasi-Reorganization" as of December 31, 1982, whereby the accumulated deficit of the Company was eliminated by a charge to additional paid-in capital. Subsequent adjustments to the recorded 1982 gain in the amount of $253,889, including a gain of $250,000 resulting from a syndicate (including an officer and a director of the Company) purchasing the shares allocated to a creditor who had asserted a claim against the Company's guarantee of certain Big Smith liabilities, have also been credited directly to additional paid-in capital in 1983.

3. Big Smith Chapter 11 Proceedings and Reorganization

On August 10, 1983, as approved by its creditors, Big Smith received confirmation of its plan of reorganization from the U.S. Bankruptcy Court. Big Smith had filed petitions for reorganization pursuant to Chapter 11 of the United States Bankruptcy Code on December 31, 1981.

• • • •

In accordance with the "Quasi-Reorganization" effected by the Company as of December 31, 1982, the Big Smith gain has been credited directly to additional paid-in capital.

• • • •

DALFORT CORPORATION AND SUBSIDIARY

Consolidated Balance Sheet

	January 31, 1984	December 31, 1982
	(in thousands)	
Stockholders' equity (deficiency) (Notes 4, 10 and 16)		
Convertible preferred stock:		
Series CC 10% noncumulative	4,920	
Series EE noncumulative	5,258	
Common stock	94	15
Additional paid-in capital	70,365	67,188
Accumulated deficit after eliminating accumulated deficit of $492,720,000 at December 15, 1983	(1,774)	(505,032)
	78,863	(437,829)

Consolidated Statement of Changes in Stockholders' Equity (Deficiency)
(in thousands)

	Preferred Stock		Common Stock $.50 Par Value	Common Stock $.01 Par Value	Paid-In Capital	Retained Earnings (Deficit)	Total
	Series CC	Series EE					
Balance, December 31, 1980			$15		$67,188	$ 12,036	$ 79,239
Net loss						(153,881)	(153,881)
Common dividend declared						(4,062)	(4,062)
Preferred dividends earned and undeclared						(8,612)	(8,612)
Balance, December 31, 1981			15		67,188	(154,519)	(87,316)
Net loss						(341,900)	(341,900)
Preferred dividends earned and undeclared						(8,613)	(8,613)
Balance, December 31, 1982			15		67,188	(505,032)	(437,829)
Net income through consummation of plan of reorganization						20,531	20,531
Preferred dividends earned and undeclared						(8,219)	(8,219)
Issuance of equity securities in settlement of net liabilities subject to Chapter 11 reorganization proceedings		5,258	(15)	14	3,177	492,720	501,154
Investment of Hyatt Air	$4,920			80			5,000
Balance at date of consummation of reorganization, December 15, 1983	4,920	5,258		94	70,365		80,637
Net loss						(1,774)	(1,774)
Balance, January 31, 1984	$4,920	$5,258		$94	$70,365	$ (1,774)	$ 78,863

See accompanying notes.

Statement of Changes in Redeemable Cumulative Preferred Stock
(in thousands)

	Series A Amount	Series B Amount	Series D Amount	Total
Balance, December 31, 1980	$ 30,150	$ 45,225	$ 35,343	$ 110,718
Preferred dividends, earned and undeclared	1,800	2,700	4,112	8,612
Balance, December 31, 1981	31,950	47,925	39,455	119,330
Preferred dividends, earned and undeclared	1,800	2,700	4,113	8,613
Balance, December 31, 1982	33,750	50,625	43,568	127,943
Preferred dividends, earned and undeclared	1,718	2,577	3,924	8,219
Shares cancelled pursuant to Plan of Reorganization	$(35,468)	$(53,202)	$(47,492)	$(136,162)

See accompanying notes.

Notes to Consolidated Financial Statements

Note 1. Reorganization Proceedings

Dalfort Corporation ("Dalfort"), formerly Braniff Airways, Incorporated ("Airways"), emerged from a proceeding for reorganization under Chapter 11 of the United States Bankruptcy Code ("Bankruptcy Code") in December 1983. In connection therewith, Dalfort formed its only subsidiary, Braniff, Inc. ("Braniff"), and in December 1983 Dalfort initially capitalized Braniff.

Following several years of unprofitable operations, Airways ceased all airline operations on May 12, 1982, and on May 13, 1982, Airways, its parent Braniff International Corporation ("International") and Braniff Realty Company ("Realty"), a then wholly-owned subsidiary of International, filed petitions for reorganization under Chapter 11 of the Bankruptcy Code.

• • • •

As described above, pursuant to the Plan, upon consummation all debts arising prior to May 13, 1982, have been (or will be) satisfied in exchange for certain amounts of cash, the transfer of certain assets to the former creditors and the issuance of preferred stock and common stock of Dalfort. In addition, Dalfort has issued or caused to be issued certain warrants to purchase the common stock of Braniff and scrip for the partial purchase of air transportation on Braniff. Dalfort has accounted for the reorganization in a manner similar to a quasi-reorganization and consequently the following adjustments were made as of December 15, 1983 (in thousands):

Liabilities extinguished, net of current assets transferred or to be transferred to former creditors of Airways	$ 583,267
Redeemable cumulative preferred stock cancelled	136,162
Acquisition of leasehold interests	4,109
Property and equipment transferred to former creditors of Airways	(203,202)
Issuance of series AA and BB convertible preferred stock	(19,182)
Net increase in stockholders' equity	$ 501,154

Note 2. Summary of Significant Accounting Policies

• • • •

Settlements With Creditors. The consummation of the Plan was accounted for in a manner similar to a quasi-reorganization. The net credit of approximately $496 million resulting from the extinguishment of liabilities and the transfer of assets and the issuance of equity securities to former creditors pursuant to the Plan was recorded as additional paid-in capital, and the accumulated deficit of approximately $492.7 million at December 15, 1983, was eliminated by a transfer to additional paid-in capital. The effects of individual settlements with creditors which were not dependent upon consummation of the Plan were recognized in determining income.

• • • •

ENERGY MANAGEMENT CORPORATION AND SUBSIDIARIES

(EMC and RIC in U.S. Chapter 11 Proceedings from February 14, 1986 to December 15, 1986)
Consolidated Balance Sheets

	December 31	
	1986	1985
STOCKHOLDERS' EQUITY (DEFICIT) (Notes 1, 3, 5 and 10):		
Class A common stock, $0.01 par value; 20,000,000 shares authorized; 8,000,000 shares issued	80	
Class B common stock, $0.01 par value; 2,000,000 shares authorized; 2,000,000 shares to be issued	20	
Preferred stock.... cancelled 12/31/86		7,666
Common stock, no par value.... cancelled 12/31/86		7,195
Capital in excess of par value (less than stated value)	4,732	(3,880)
Retained earnings (accumulated deficit)		(34,409)
	4,832	(23,428)

Consolidated Statements of Stockholders' Equity (Deficit)
Three Years Ended December 31, 1986

	Common Stock Stated Value	Preferred Stock Stated Value	Capital in Excess of Par Value	Retained Earnings (Accumulated Deficit)	Common Stock	
					Class A	Class B
Balance, December 31, 1983	$4,731		$ 1,244	$(12,290)		
Net loss				(11,051)		
Issuance of common stock in exchange for 12% Senior Convertible Subordinated Debentures (Note 5)	2,367		1,006			
Issuance of preferred stock (Note 5):						
Past due interest in connection with exchange offer		$1,996	(998)			
Payment of interest		3,055	(2,335)			
Other				10		
Balance, December 31, 1984	7,098	5,051	(1,083)	(23,331)		
Net loss				(11,078)		
Issuance of preferred stock for payment of interest		2,819	(2,653)			

Consolidated Statements of Stockholders' Equity (Deficit) (continued)
Three Years Ended December 31, 1986

	Common Stock Stated Value	Preferred Stock Stated Value	Capital in Excess of Par Value	Retained Earnings (Accumulated Deficit)	Common Stock Class A	Class B
Conversion of preferred stock to common stock	67	(204)	137			
Cancellation of treasury stock	(458)					
Issuance of common stock in settlement of litigation	500		(438)			
Other	(12)					
Balance, December 31, 1985	$7,195	$7,666	(3,880)	$(34,409)		
Net loss				(3,257)		
Conversion of preferred stock to common stock	109	(359)	250			
Issuance of common stock pursuant to estate redemption of the 15% participating investment certificate	227		(207)			
Other	2	25	4			
Cancellation of common stock and preferred stock pursuant to the Plan	(7,534)	(7,332)	14,866			
Elimination of public debt, bank debt, and other prepetition liabilities pursuant to the Plan			31,465			
Elimination of accumulated deficit pursuant to the Plan			(37,666)	37,666		
Class A common stock issued and Class B common stock to be issued pursuant to the Plan			(100)		$80	$20
Balance December 31, 1986	$ 0	$ 0	$4,732	$ 0	$80	$20

Notes to Consolidated Financial Statements

1. The Company

Background. Since 1968 Energy Management Corporation ("EMC") and subsidiaries have been engaged in exploration for, and production of, oil and gas in the continental United States principally through affiliated public drilling programs organized under the name Energy Gas & Oil Drilling

Programs. EMC has two wholly owned subsidiaries, Resources Investment Corporation ("RIC") and Resources Capital Corporation ("RCC"). In addition, EMC owns 95% of Energy Coal Corporation ("ECC"). EMC, RIC, RCC and ECC are Colorado corporations. Effective January 1, 1980, EMC acquired majority ownership in all of its partnerships formed through 1978 along with majority ownership in five previously unaffiliated limited partnerships. At December 31, 1984, all partnerships formed through 1978 were dissolved. In addition, at December 31, 1984, EMC dissolved three partnerships formed during 1979 and 1980. At June 30, 1985, three additional partnerships formed between 1979 and 1981 were dissolved. At December 31, 1986, EMC dissolved its three remaining oil and gas partnerships formed during 1981 and 1982. No public programs have been organized since 1982.

• • • •

Since 1983, EMC has experienced significant financial difficulties. As a result thereof, EMC and RIC individually filed voluntary Chapter 11 petitions in the United States Bankruptcy Court for the District of Colorado ("Bankruptcy Court") on February 14, 1986. EMC and RIC emerged from Chapter 11 bankruptcy following confirmation of an Amended Joint Plan of Reorganization ("Plan") by the Bankruptcy Court on December 15, 1986. Pursuant to the Plan, Tomlinson Oil Co., Inc. ("Tomlinson") acquired 80% ownership of EMC. Tomlinson is owned 80% by R.D. Smith Group Holdings, Inc. (See Notes 3 and 9).

On December 31, 1986, EMC completed its reorganization for financial statement purposes whereby the accumulated deficit at that date was eliminated against capital in excess of par value. Accordingly, retained earnings subsequent to December 31, 1986 will reflect the activities of EMC beginning January 1, 1987. In addition, accumulated depreciation, depletion and amortization at December 31, 1986 was eliminated against the original costs of the assets.

• • • •

ITEL CORPORATION AND SUBSIDIARIES

Consolidated Balance Sheet
December 31, 1983 and 1982
(in thousands)

	1983	1982
Common stockholders' equity (deficit):		
Common stock	14,500	12,100
Capital surplus	68,100	95,200
Accumulated deficit		(320,400)
Accumulated deficit from September 19, 1983	(2,100)	
Total common stockholders' equity (deficit)	80,500	(213,100)

Consolidated Statement of Common Stockholders' Equity
Years Ended December 31, 1983, 1982, and 1981
(in thousands)

	Common Stock	Capital Surplus	Accumulated Deficit
Balance at December 31, 1982	12,100	95,200	(320,400)
Vesting under restricted stock bonus plan	100	300	
Net income through September 18, 1983			18,700
Reorganization	2,300	(27,400)	301,700
Net loss for the period September 19, 1983 to December 31, 1983			(1,000)
Amortization of preferred stock discount			(1,100)
Balance at December 31, 1983	$14,500	$68,100	$ (2,100)

Notes to Consolidated Financial Statements

• • • •

Note 2. Reorganization

The reorganized Itel Corporation is structured principally as a holding company with operating subsidiaries. The assets formerly utilized by Itel Corporation's Rail Division, including four short-line railroads, railcars owned by Itel Corporation and $6 million in cash were transferred to a new subsidiary, Itel Rail Corporation ("Itel Rail"). Itel Rail now conducts all of the Company's rail operations (except for the management and marketing of the Company's residual interests in rail-related assets managed by the Portfolio Management Division) and will continue to operate the Company's railroad equipment leasing business.

Another new subsidiary, Itel Container Corporation ("Itel Container"), owns all of the assets formerly owned by Itel Corporation's Container Division (other than the stock of certain affiliates). A second new container subsidiary, Itel Containers International Corporation ("Containers International"), succeeded to the assets and operations of Itel Container International B.V., the Netherlands corporation through which the Company previously conducted its container leasing business.

• • • •

Reclassifications and Adjustments. Together with the distribution of cash and securities, certain adjustments and reclassifications were recorded to give effect to the reorganization. A provision of $53.3 million has been made to reduce Itel Corporation's investment in Itel Rail to zero because of significant uncertainties regarding the timing and amount of future cash flows from Itel Rail to Itel Corporation. The adjustment will result in a reduction in future depreciation expense through amortization over the estimated remaining life of the rail assets. The projections for the period through 1987, on which the Plan was partly based, indicate that cash generated by Itel Rail is not expected to be sufficient to permit payment of dividends to Itel Corporation based upon the cash flows and the restrictions on dividends imposed by the ETC Modification Agreement.

The following table shows the effect of these adjustments on common stockholders' equity (in thousands).

Common stockholders' deficit at September 19, 1983 prior to reorganization	$(194,000)
Reorganization adjustments:	
Recognition of claims in the reorganization proceeding which resulted from rejection of executory contracts and resolution of disputed claims	(42,400)
Excess of unsecured claims and interests over face amount of cash payments and distribution of reorganization securities (i.e. debt forgiveness)	293,100
Discount applied to 14% Secured Notes, 10% Notes, and New Redeemable Preferred Stock (see Notes 9 and 14)	88,500
Write-off of debt discount associated with pre-Petition unsecured claims	(9,300)
Reduction of investment in Itel Rail	(53,300)
Common stockholders' equity at September 19, 1983 post-reorganization	$ 82,600

Common Stockholders' Equity. In addition to the adjustments described above, the common stockholders' equity accounts were adjusted to eliminate the accumulated deficit at the Effective Date.

• • • •

MAGIC CIRCLE ENERGY CORPORATION AND SUBSIDIARY

Consolidated Balance Sheets

	December 31	
	1986	1985
STOCKHOLDERS' EQUITY (Notes F and K)		
Common stock—authorized 25,000,000 shares of $.10 par value; issued and outstanding 12,969,626 shares	1,297	1,297
Additional paid-in capital	1,561	10,317
Accumulated deficit before December 31, 1986		(9,302)
Retained earnings at December 31, 1986		
Total stockholders' equity	2,858	2,312

Consolidated Statements of Stockholders' Equity
(Based on full cost method of accounting)

	Common Stock	Additional Paid-In Capital	Retained Earnings (Accumulated Deficit)
• • • •			
Balance at December 31, 1985	1,297	10,317	(9,302)
Net earnings for the year			546
Accumulated deficit adjusted in reorganization (Note F)		(8,756)	(8,756)
Balance at December 31, 1986	$1,297	$ 1,561	$ 0

Notes to Consolidated Financial Statements
December 31, 1986, 1985, and 1984

• • • •

Note B. Bankruptcy Proceedings and Reorganization Plans

On July 15, 1986, the Company, Wells Fargo Bank, N.A., and the Unsecured Creditors' Committee for Magic Circle Energy Corporation filed a Joint Plan of Reorganization which was confirmed on September 9, 1986. An amendment to the Plan was approved September 30, 1986. The Plan became effective on February 28, 1987.

The Plan calls for the Company to retain its oil shale property, drilling rigs, $500,000 of cash, and its 100% owned subsidiary, Congress Consolidated Gold Mining Corporation (the Retained Assets). A new limited partnership (the Partnership), with the Company as the sole limited partner and a newly-formed subsidiary of the Company as the sole general partner, was formed pursuant to this plan. All assets other than those retained, together with all debts not satisfied by cash payments, were transferred to the Partnership.

• • • •

Note F. Reorganization

As a result of the reorganization and to reflect the reorganized status of the Company, the accumulated deficit as of December 31, 1986, has been eliminated by a transfer to additional paid-in capital.

• • • •

MEGO CORP. AND SUBSIDIARIES

Consolidated Balance Sheets

	February 29, 1984	February 28, 1983
		(unaudited)
Common stock and other shareholders' (deficiency) (notes 1a, 2 and 5)		
Common stock, $.10 par value—authorized 10,000,000 shares; issued and outstanding 2,752,900 shares		275
Common stock, Class A, $.01 par value—authorized 12,200,000 shares; issued and outstanding 9,113,522 shares	91	
Common stock, Class B, $.01 par value—authorized 1,200,000 shares; issued and outstanding 1,169,176 shares	11	
Additional paid-in capital		4,390
Accumulated (deficit):		
Prior to December 1, 1983	(1,410)	(57,994)
After December 1, 1983	(59)	
	(1,367)	(53,329)
Less: Common stock subscribed (note 5)	63	
Total shareholders' (deficiency)	(1,430)	(53,329)

Consolidated Statements of Changes in Common Stock and Other Shareholders' Equity (Deficiency)
(Notes 1a, 2 and 5)
(unaudited)

	Common Stock No Par Value	Class A $.01 Par Value	Class B $.01 Par Value	Additional Paid-In Capital	Accumulated (Deficit)	Common Stock Subscribed
Balance at March 1, 1981	$226			$ 4,390	$ (8,022)	
Net loss					(22,916)	
Balance at February 28, 1982	226			4,390	(30,938)	
Common shares issued	48					
Net loss					(27,055)	
Balance at February 28, 1983	275			4,390	(57,994)	
Common shares issued		$54		1,147		
Common shares issued in exchange for old shares (Class B)	(275)		$ 3	272		
Common shares issued for indebtedness		36	8	55,448		
Common stock subscribed (Class A)						$(63)
Effect of quasi-reorganization				(61,258)	61,258	
Net loss					(4,733)	
Balance at February 29, 1984	$ 0	$91	$11	$ 0	$ (1,469)	$(63)

Notes to Consolidated Financial Statements

Note 1. Summary of Significant Accounting Policies

a. Chapter XI Proceedings and Quasi-Reorganization. On June 14, 1982 Mego International, Inc. ("International") and its principal domestic operating subsidiary, Mego Corp., filed petitions for Reorganization under Chapter XI of the United States Bankruptcy Code with the Bankruptcy Court for the Southern District of New York. On November 9, 1983, an order was entered by the Bankruptcy Court confirming a Plan of Reorganization (the "Plan") (see Note 2) of International and Mego Corp. On December 1, 1983, pursuant to the Plan, International was merged into Mego Corp. (the "Merger") and International's issued and outstanding common stock was cancelled and converted into the right to receive shares of Mego Corp.'s common stock. In addition, all of the new common and preferred stock of Mego Corp. was issued in satisfaction of claims.

Mego Corp. has accounted for the Plan of Reorganization as a quasi-reorganization at November 30, 1983. Accordingly, $61,258,612 of deficit has been offset against additional paid-in-capital. The deficit exceeded additional paid-in-capital at November 30, 1983, by $1,410,269.

• • • •

PANEX INDUSTRIES, INC. AND SUBSIDIARIES

Consolidated Balance Sheets
as of October 2, 1983 and October 3, 1982

	1983	1982
STOCKHOLDERS' EQUITY—Notes 3, 6 and 8		
Common Stock, par value $.10 per share. Authorized 4,000,000 shares, issued 1,844,202 shares	184	184
Capital in excess of par	40,825	36,146
Retained earnings from June 4, 1981 (date of reorganization)	11,914	6,608
Common Stock held in treasury, at cost—3,504 and 1,619 shares	(45)	(19)
TOTAL STOCKHOLDERS' EQUITY	52,878	42,919

Consolidated Statements of Stockholders' Equity (Deficiency)
for the Years Ended October 2, 1983, October 3, 1982, and September 27, 1981

	Common Stock $.10 Par Value	Preferred Stock Series B	Common Stock $.75 Par Value	Capital in Excess of Par	(Deficit)	Retained Earnings From June 4, 1981	Common Stock Held in Treasury
Balance at September 28, 1980		$83	$2,599	$39,249	$(26,313)		$(20,038)
Cancellation of issued shares pursuant to Plan of Reorganization—Note 8		(83)	(2,599)	(17,356)			20,038
Distribution of 2,714,861 shares of new common stock to creditors pursuant to Plan of Reorganization valued at $10 per share—Note 8	$271			26,878			
Net income—Note 8					17,952	$ 2,243	
Elimination of deficit at June 4, 1981 against capital in excess of par in connection with reorganization—Note 8				(8,361)	8,361		
Benefit from use of net operating loss carryforward after reorganization—Note 4				2,000			

Consolidated Statements of Stockholders' Equity (Deficiency) (continued)
for the Years Ended October 2, 1983, October 3, 1982, and September 27, 1981

	Common Stock $.10 Par Value	Preferred Stock Series B	Common Stock $.75 Par Value	Capital in Excess of Par	(Deficit)	Retained Earnings From June 4, 1981	Common Stock Held in Treasury
Balance at September 27, 1981	271			42,410		2,243	
Acquisition of 872,278 shares of common stock of which 870,659 shares were retired and 1,619 shares were held in treasury— Note 3	(87)			(10,429)			(19)
Net income						4,365	
Benefit from use of net operating and capital loss carryforwards— Note 4				4,165			
Balance at October 3, 1982	184			36,146		6,608	(19)
Net income						5,582	
Acquisition of 1,885 shares of common stock held in treasury— Note 3							(26)
Dividends declared ($.15 per share)						(276)	
Benefit from use of net operating and capital loss carryforwards— Note 4				4,679			
BALANCE AT OCTOBER 2, 1983	$184	$ 0	$ 0	$40,825	$ 0	$11,914	$ (45)

Notes to Consolidated Financial Statements

• • • •

Note 8. Plan of Reorganization and Discharge From Chapter X of the Bankruptcy Act

On August 31, 1976, The Duplan Corporation ("Duplan") and one subsidiary, Duplan Fabrics, Inc. ("Fabrics"), filed petitions for arrangement under Chapter XI of the Bankruptcy Act (the "Act") in the United States District Court for the Southern District of New York (the "Court"). On October 5, 1976, the Chapter XI cases were transferred to Chapter X of the Act, and a Reorganization Trustee ("Trustee") was appointed.

On June 4, 1981, the Court confirmed a Plan of Reorganization ("Plan") which had been proposed by the Trustee and accepted by a majority of affected creditors. Duplan and Fabrics were thereupon discharged from bankruptcy, a new Board of Directors was appointed and Duplan's name was changed to Panex Industries, Inc. ("Panex"). On June 15, 1981, a Restated Certificate of Incorporation was filed which changed the classes of securities which Panex is authorized to issue to 4,000,000 shares of Common Stock, par value $.10 per share.

• • • •

The effect of the settlement of liabilities upon discharge from bankruptcy, net of legal and other administrative expenses of $3,760,000 incurred during the reorganization proceedings, is reflected as an extraordinary credit of $8,990,000 in the accompanying consolidated statement of income for the year ended September 27, 1981. Pursuant to a ruling received from the Internal Revenue Service, the gain on settlement does not represent taxable income. The extraordinary credit includes a tax benefit of $900,000 related to a portion of administrative expenses estimated to be deductible for tax purposes. In March 1982, the Court awarded fees to the successor debenture trustee in excess of the amount previously accrued therefor in fiscal 1981. Principally as a result thereof, an additional $470,000 of administrative expenses has been recorded as an extraordinary charge in the accompanying consolidated statement of income for the year ended October 3, 1982.

For financial reporting purposes, as a result of the reorganization and to reflect the reorganized status of Panex, the deficit as of June 4, 1981, has been extinguished by a charge to capital in excess of par and earnings subsequent to such date have been shown as retained earnings arising after the date of reorganization.

• • • •

STORAGE TECHNOLOGY CORPORATION

Consolidated Balance Sheet
(in thousands)

	December 25, 1987	December 26, 1986
Stockholders' equity (deficit):		
• • • •		
Common stock, $.01 par value, 293,000,000 shares authorized and 228,089,671 shares issued in 1957; $.10 par value, 60,000,000 shares authorized and 34,759,892 shares issued in 1986	2,280	3,476
Capital in excess of par value	226,843	260,926
Retained earnings (from June 26, 1987)	4,472	
Accumulated deficit[1]		(282,233)
Less: Treasury shares of 14,760 in 1987 and 14,563 in 1986	(230)	(229)
Total stockholders' equity (deficit)	233,365	(18,060)

[1]A retained earnings deficit of $265,030 was eliminated at June 26, 1987 in connection with a quasi-reorganization. (See Note 2)

Consolidated Statement of Changes in Stockholders' Equity (Deficit)
(in thousands)

	Common Stock	Capital in Excess of Par Value	Retained Earnings (Deficit)	Treasury Stock (at Cost)
Balances, December 28, 1984	$3,458	$260,546	$(260,976)	$228
Proceeds from sales of common stock— Employee stock purchase plan	11	205		
Net loss			(57,437)	
Balances, December 27, 1985	3,469	260,751	(318,413)	228
Proceeds from sales of common stock— Stock options	7	175		
Shares surrendered to exercise stock options				1
Net income			36,180	

Consolidated Statement of Changes in Stockholders' Equity (Deficit) (continued)
(in thousands)

	Common Stock	Capital in Excess of Par Value	Retained Earnings (Deficit)	Treasury Stock (at Cost)
Balances, December 26, 1986	3,476	260,926	(282,233)	229
Proceeds from sales of common stock— Stock options	8	338		
Shares surrendered to exercise stock options				1
Shares distributed in connection with reorganization (Note 2)	1,925	223,147		
Adjustment of common stock to $.01 par value (Note 2)	(3,129)	3,129		
Elimination of accumulated deficit at June 26, 1987 (Note 2)		(265,030)	265,030	
Net income			26,008	
Reclassification of pre-quasi-reorganization net operating loss benefits (Note 13)		4,333	(4,333)	
Balances, December 25, 1987	$2,280	$226,843	$ 4,472	$230

Notes to Consolidated Financial Statements

• • • •

Note 2. Emergence From Chapter 11 Reorganization

In October 1984 and May 1986, Storage Technology Corporation and substantially all of its United States subsidiaries filed separate voluntary petitions for reorganization under Chapter 11 of the United States Bankruptcy Code (Chapter 11). The Company continued to operate the business as debtors-in-possession subject to the control and supervision of the United States Bankruptcy Court (Bankruptcy Court).

• • • •

In accordance with the Plan, StorageTek distributed approximately $187,000,000 in cash, $285,000,000 in 13.5% Senior debentures (see Note 12) and approximately 193,000,000 shares of common stock in satisfaction of approximately $860,000,000 of priority and unsecured claims and administrative expenses. The recorded liabilities so liquidated were approximately $706,000,000. In addition, the Company allowed approximately $93,000,000 of secured claims related to nonrecourse borrowings and allowed the reinstatement or survival of additional debt arrangements of approximately $20,000,000.

The Company has accounted for the distribution as a quasi-reorganization. Goodwill (representing the excess of the fair value of the securities and cash distributed over the book value of the discharged liabilities) was not recorded since management believes it to be inappropriate to reflect goodwill in connection with emergence from bankruptcy reorganization proceedings. Capital stock at par value of $1,925,000 and Capital in excess of par value of $223,147,000 were recorded in connection with the quasi-reorganization. The sum of these amounts represents the difference between a) book liabilities discharged, and b) Plan cash, debentures and liabilities accrued pursuant to the reorganization. In accordance with quasi-reorganization accounting provisions, the Accumulated deficit of $265,030,000 at June 26, 1987, was reclassified against Capital in excess of par value.

• • • •

Note 4. Extraordinary Gain

During the second quarter of 1986, StorageTek renegotiated an executory contract with a supplier. The settlement, approved by the Bankruptcy Court, provided for, among other provisions, the forgiveness of a portion of StorageTek's payable to the supplier. Accordingly, an extraordinary gain of $2,595,000, net of taxes of $2,396,000, representing the debt forgiveness was recorded. The balance of the payable was converted to an administrative claim, a portion of which was paid upon settlement and a substantial portion was paid in installments in conjunction with the payment of ongoing purchases of inventory from the supplier. The balance remaining at December 25, 1987, was converted to a general unsecured claim and credited to Capital in excess of par value in accordance with quasi-reorganization accounting (Note 2). The general unsecured claim will be paid with cash and reorganization securities held by a trustee and reserved for such purposes.

• • • •

Note 14. Employee Benefit Plans and Options

• • • •

Stock Option Plans.

• • • •

In 1985, employment and retention agreements were issued to certain officers and key employees which provided for, among other things, the issuance of stock options upon the successful reorganization of the Company. In July 1987, pursuant to these agreements, options to purchase 7,900,000 shares were granted at the then current market price of $2.75 (the $2.75 options) and options to purchase 4,700,000 shares were granted at option prices ranging from $.34 to $.52 per share (employment agreement options). Compensation associated with the latter options that were granted at less than the current market price was charged to Capital in excess of par value in connection with the quasi-reorganization.

• • • •

IV

ASSETS (BUT NOT LIABILITIES) RESTATED

Some companies that applied quasi-reorganizations restated some or all assets at the time of the quasi-reorganization without restating liabilities. Thirteen examples of such companies are presented below. Although one of the companies mentioned restated liabilities, it did not provide such accounting entries in connection with the quasi-reorganization. The examples are classified according to whether or not the company was being reorganized in a bankruptcy proceeding at the time of the quasi-reorganization.

NOT UNDER BANKRUPTCY PROCEEDING

BLOCKER ENERGY CORPORATION AND SUBSIDIARIES

Consolidated Balance Sheets

	December 31	
	1984	1983
	(in thousands)	
SHAREHOLDERS' EQUITY (Notes 3 and 6):		
Common stock, $.10 par value; 45,000,000 shares authorized, 33,434,602 and 33,320,602 shares, respectively, issued and outstanding	3,343	3,332
Additional paid-in capital	58,177	57,778
Retained earnings (deficit), since elimination of deficit of $113,448,000 at December 31, 1983	(11,883)	
Cumulative translation adjustment	170	
	49,807	61,110

Consolidated Statements of Shareholders' Equity (Deficit)
(Notes 1 and 2)

	Common Stock Amount	Additional Paid-In Capital	Retained Earnings (Deficit)	Cumulative Translation Adjustment
		(in thousands)		
BALANCE—December 31, 1982	600	31,566	(54,313)	
Exercise of employee stock options		14		
Assignment of minority interest shares of Canadian subsidiary (Note 6)		780		
Cumulative translation adjustment:				
As of January 1, 1983				(1,892)
Change during 1983				(31)
Net loss			(59,135)	
Issuance of stock and adjustments to effect debt restructuring and corporate recapitalization	2,732	25,418	113,448	1,923
BALANCE—December 31, 1983	3,332	57,778		

Notes to Consolidated Financial Statements

• • • •

2. Debt Restructuring and Corporate Recapitalization

• • • •

On March 22, 1984, the shareholders of the Company approved the debt restructuring plan and a proposal to increase the authorized shares of common stock. Additionally, the Board of Directors of the Company approved a corporate recapitalization effective December 31, 1983, concurrently with the debt restructuring.

The following table sets forth the consolidated balance sheet of the Company as of December 31, 1983, prior to debt restructuring and as adjusted to give effect to the debt restructuring and corporate recapitalization described herein.

	Balance Sheet—December 31, 1983		
	Prior to Debt Restructuring and Corporate Recapitalization	Adjustments	As Adjusted for Debt Restructuring and Corporate Recapitalization
	(in thousands except per share amounts)		

• • • •

SHAREHOLDERS' EQUITY (DEFICIT):
Preferred stock, 2,000,000 shares authorized; none issued or outstanding

	Prior to Debt Restructuring and Corporate Recapitalization	Adjustments	As Adjusted for Debt Restructuring and Corporate Recapitalization
Common stock $.10 par value, 20,000,000 shares authorized at December 31, 1983, 45,000,000 shares as adjusted; 6,005,313 shares issued and outstanding at December 31, 1983, 33,320,602 shares as adjusted	600	2,152[a]	3,332
		339[c]	
		176[d]	
		65[e]	

	Balance Sheet—December 31, 1983 *(continued)*		
	Prior to Debt Restructuring and Corporate Recapitalization	Adjustments	As Adjusted for Debt Restructuring and Corporate Recapitalization
	(in thousands except per share amounts)		
Cumulative translation adjustment	(1,923)	(1,923)[h]	
Additional paid-in capital	32,360	124,583[a]	57,778
		9,333[c]	
		6,196[d]	
		3,175[e]	
		(2,498)[g]	
		(115,371)[h]	
Retained earnings (deficit)	(113,448)	113,448[h]	
Total Shareholders' Equity (Deficit)	(82,411)	143,521	61,110
Total Liabilities and Shareholders' Equity (Deficit)	$156,492	$ (4,730)	$151,762

• • • •

Adjustments were made to the Company's December 31, 1983, balance sheet prior to the restructuring to reflect (1) consummation of the debt restructuring and (2) a corporate recapitalization. The Company believes that, because of the debt restructuring, it is again a viable competitor in the international contract drilling industry. It is further believed that, when the significant changes in the Company's capitalization resulting from the restructuring are considered with the Company's previous withdrawal from oil and gas exploration and development activities and cancellation of the delivery of a submersible drilling rig, a corporate recapitalization was necessary to reflect properly the Company's financial condition on a post-restructuring basis. A corporate recapitalization is an optional, as opposed to mandatory, accounting procedure and is intended to restate assets and liabilities to their current values, eliminate the deficit in retained earnings and provide a "new beginning" from an accounting and financial reporting standpoint.

The Company removed certain component parts from four of its land rigs which its management believed to be noncompetitive for future use as spare parts for other of its rigs. The remaining components of those four rigs were sold at auction in November 1984. Accordingly, the carrying value of those components sold was reduced to their anticipated realizable value.

No other adjustment has been made to the carrying value of the Company's drilling rigs and equipment because the Company believes that the book value of such equipment is essentially the same as or below its fair market value, defined as the price which would be paid by a willing buyer to a willing seller in a non-distress exchange. Because substantially all recent sales of drilling equipment have been at auctions resulting from creditor foreclosures or business failures, the fair market value (as so defined) for drilling equipment is not readily available. It appears that much of the equipment sold recently has been sold to investors, rather than drilling contractors, who believe the underlying value of the equipment is substantially greater than the price paid in such distress sales. The Company has made inquiries of professional equipment appraisers, rig manufacturers, major banks and other industry experts as to rig values and concluded, based on the considerations discussed above, that there should be no revaluation of its other equipment as part of a corporate recapitalization.

The adjustments to reflect the debt restructuring and corporate recapitalization are as follows:

a. To reflect the exchange of secured notes with a fair value of $60,359,000 (based on a face value of $80,000,000 and a discount of $19,641,000 resulting from interest for the first 2½ years at below market rates) and common stock for secured notes in the total principal amount of $160,000,000 and related accrued and deferred interest.

b. To reflect amendment of the line of credit, which was to have been payable in June 1984, to make it payable in 1993.

c. To reflect the exchange of notes and common stock in settlement of accrued and future lease obligations relating to four marine drilling barges and the exchange of common stock in settlement of such lease obligations relating to a fifth barge. In connection with the issuance of such notes, $4,885,000 has been recorded as drilling rigs and related equipment to reflect the classification of the four barges as capital assets. Additionally, $932,000 of unamortized deferred gains relating to the original sale and leaseback arrangements on certain of these barges has been credited to additional paid-in capital (see Note 4).

d. To reflect exchanges through October 12, 1984, of common stock and warrants for $5,855,000 principal amount of outstanding subordinated debentures and the related accrued interest. The unamortized deferred offering costs relating to such debentures ($207,000) were charged to additional paid-in capital. Subsequent to October 12, 1984, an additional $380,000 principal amount of debentures were exchanged. The effects of such exchanges have been accounted for as adjustments to the exchange offer in 1984 (see Note 10).

e. To reflect the exchange of a $2,000,000 note and common stock for an existing $4,000,000 note on which interest of $750,000 had accrued, and the discount to fair value resulting from the below-market interest rate on such $2,000,000 note.

f. To eliminate deferred income taxes attributable to drilling rigs and related equipment and to reflect such assets net of related future tax liabilities.

g. To reduce to expected net realizable value ($500,000) the carrying value of four noncompetitive drilling rigs sold at auction in 1984. The Company retained certain equipment from the rigs to be used as separate parts, totaling $920,000 out of the total net book value of $3,918,000.

h. To eliminate the deficit in retained earnings and the cumulative translation adjustment resulting from the election to effect a corporate recapitalization.

• • • •

CALLON PETROLEUM COMPANY

Consolidated Balance Sheets

	December 31	
	1987	1986
		(Note 1)
Shareholders' equity:		
Common stock, $.01 par value; 20,000,000 shares authorized; 9,396,633 and 9,168,522 shares issued and outstanding at December 31, 1987 and 1986, respectively	93	91
Paid-in capital in excess of par value (Note 1)	9,109	26,403
Retained earnings (deficit) (eliminated as of December 31, 1987, date of quasi-reorganization) (Note 1)		(66,598)
Total shareholders' equity (deficit)	9,203	(40,104)

Consolidated Statement of Shareholders' Equity
(Note 1)

	Common Stock	Paid-In Capital in Excess of Par Value	Retained Earnings (Deficit)
Balances, December 31, 1986	$91	$26,403	$(66,598)
Shares issued in connection with:			
Employees' stock ownership plan	7	83	
Exercise of stock options	2		
Other		17	
Shares acquired and retired by the Company	(5)	(200)	
Net income (loss) available for common stock			(2,892)
Adjustments related to quasi-reorganization (Note 1):			
Impact of settlements and restructurings pursuant to quasi-reorganization (Note 1)			52,293
Transfer of accumulated deficit as of December 31, 1987 to paid-in capital in excess of par value (Note 1)		(17,197)	17,197
Balances, December 31, 1987	$93	$ 9,109	$ 0

Notes to Consolidated Financial Statements

1. Corporate Reorganization

• • • •

Quasi-Reorganization. The Board of Directors of the Company has directed that, effective December 31, 1987, the Company undergo a quasi-reorganization. A quasi-reorganization is an elective accounting procedure intended to restate assets and liabilities to current values and eliminate any accumulated deficit in retained earnings.

Accordingly, the various debt and preferred stock settlements and other reorganizations that occurred during 1987 have been accounted for as direct shareholders' equity transactions, rather than as results of operations, and the Company's accumulated deficit as of December 31, 1987 ($17,197,715) has been eliminated against Paid-in Capital in Excess of Par Value.

The impact on shareholders' equity of the settlement and reorganization transactions described above was as follows:

1. FDIC Settlement and Formation of Callon Consolidated Partners, L.P.

Cancellation of debt and accrued interest owed to FDIC	$55,403,160
Transfer of liabilities to Callon Consolidated Partners, L.P.	7,570,590
Transfer of gas balancing liability to FDIC	1,474,468
Carrying value of oil and gas properties transferred	(27,898,638)
	$36,549,580

2. Industrial Development Revenue Bond Settlement

Debt and accrued interest	$ 3,659,510
Settlement proceeds paid to holder	(850,000)
Writedown of building to fair market value	(2,809,510)

3. Callon Energy Services, Inc. Settlement

Elimination of deficit investment in subsidiary	1,930,195

4. Series A Preferred Stock Redemption

Preferred stock issue and unpaid cumulative dividends	$14,160,000
Settlement proceeds paid to preferred shareholders	(1,000,000)
	13,160,000

5. Other Secured and Unsecured Settlements

Net amount of debt and unpaid interest settled over amount of settlement proceeds and carrying value of assets returned to creditors	654,139
Impact of settlements and restructuring pursuant to quasi-reorganization	$52,293,914

The December 31, 1987, unaudited pro forma consolidated statement of operations of Callon Petroleum Company reflecting the reorganizational transactions as if they occurred as of the beginning of the year is summarized below:

Callon Petroleum Company
Pro Forma Consolidated Statement of Operations
for the Year Ended December 31, 1987
(Unaudited)

Revenues:	
Oil and gas sales	$1,486,000
Interest income	505,000
	1,991,000
Costs and expenses:	
Lease operating expenses	443,000
Depreciation, depletion and amortization of oil and gas properties	270,000
General, administrative, and technical	673,000
Interest	106,000
	1,492,000
Income before provision for income taxes	$ 499,000
Working capital provided from operations	$1,146,000

• • • •

ELECTRONIC ASSOCIATES, INC. AND SUBSIDIARIES

Consolidated Balance Sheet
(in thousands)

	December 31, 1985	December 28, 1984
Shareowners' Equity (Deficit) (Notes 2 and 5):		
• • • •		
Common stock, $1.00 par value; authorized 5,000,000 shares; outstanding 2,845,565 shares in 1985 and 2,844,565 shares in 1984	2,846	2,845
Additional paid-in capital	6,588	28,080
Accumulated deficit		(31,688)
TOTAL SHAREOWNERS' EQUITY	$9,434	$ (763)

Consolidated Statement of Shareowners' Equity
for the Three Years Ended December 31, 1985
(in thousands)

	Common Stock	Additional Paid-In Capital	Retained Earnings (Deficit)
Balance, December 28, 1984	$2,845	$28,080	$(31,688)
Net Income			1,641
Shares Issued upon exercise of Stock Options	1	3	
Quasi-Reorganization Adjustments (Note 2)		8,552	
Transfer of Accumulated Deficit to Additional Paid-In Capital (Note 2)		(30,047)	30,047
Balance, December 31, 1985	$2,846	$ 6,588	

Notes to Consolidated Financial Statements

1. Summary of Significant Accounting Policies

Revaluation of the Balance Sheet. The balance sheet at December 31, 1985 has been revalued to fair value in accordance with accounting principles applicable to quasi-reorganizations (see Note 2). The revalued balance sheet amounts represent the new cost basis for the Company.

2. Quasi-Reorganization

As of the close of business December 31, 1985, the Company effected a quasi-reorganization whereby assets were restated to their estimated current values, income postponed to future periods was reflected in shareowners' equity and the accumulated deficit was transferred to additional paid-in capital. The Board of Directors had previously determined that it would be in the best interest of the Company to implement the quasi-reorganization. The adjustments made as a result of the quasi-reorganization had no effect on the Company's cash flows or tax basis, but result in a balance sheet which better reflects the Company's financial position.

The following adjustments were made in conjunction with the quasi-reorganization: (in thousands)

Reduce carrying value of inventories	$ (243)
Reduce carrying value of property and equipment	(855)
Reclassify income postponed to future periods	10,198
Other	(548)
Total quasi-reorganization adjustments	8,552
Transfer of accumulated deficit to additional paid-in capital	(30,047)
Net transfer to additional paid-in capital	$(21,495)

• • • •

4. Leases

• • • •

Operating Leases. The Company entered into a sale and leaseback of its West Long Branch facility in December 1983. The facility has been leased back for a period of twenty years at a rental of $1,750,000 per year for the first ten years and $2,250,000 per year for the second ten years, plus a payment of $900,000 per year on account of operating expenses. The gain of $11,176,000 on the sale was deferred to be amortized in proportion to the related rental over the lease term. In connection with the quasi-reorganization, the unamortized deferred gain at December 31, 1985 was transferred to shareowners' equity (see Note 2). The Company may repurchase the property after twelve years at fair market value.

• • • •

FLUOR CORPORATION

Consolidated Balance Sheet
(in thousands at October 31)

	1987	1986
Shareholders' Equity		
Capital Stock		

• • • •

	1987	1986
Common—authorized 150,000,000 shares of $.62 ½ par value; issued and outstanding in 1987— 78,939,846 shares and in 1986—79,271,954 shares	49,337	49,545
Additional capital (1987 reflects quasi-reorganization)	487,435	1,070,845
Deficit (1987 reflects quasi-reorganization)		(160,022)
Unamortized executive stock plan expense	(4,367)	(6,736)
Cumulative translation adjustments	(662)	(3,392)
Total shareholders' equity	531,743	950,240

Consolidated Statement of Shareholders' Equity
Years Ended October 31, 1985, 1986, and 1987
(in thousands, except per share amounts)

	Common Stock	Additional Capital	Retained Earnings (Deficit)	Unamortized Executive Stock Plan Expense	Cumulative Translation Adjustments
Balances at October 31, 1984	$49,341	$1,067,549	$597,007	$(10,310)	$(7,224)
Net loss			(633,324)		
Cash dividends ($.40 per share)			(31,561)		
Exercise of stock options, net	81	1,182			
Amortization of executive stock plan expense				1,838	
Issuance of restricted stock, net	40	893		(957)	
Translation adjustment for the period					(651)
Balances at October 31, 1985	49,462	1,069,624	(67,878)	(9,429)	(7,875)
Net loss			(60,443)		
Cash dividends ($.40 per share)			(31,701)		

Consolidated Statement of Shareholders' Equity (continued)
Years Ended October 31, 1985, 1986, and 1987
(in thousands, except per share amounts)

	Common Stock	Additional Capital	Retained Earnings (Deficit)	Unamortized Executive Stock Plan Expense	Cumulative Translation Adjustments
Exercise of stock options, net	67	991			
Amortization of executive stock plan expense				3,303	
Issuance of restricted stock, net	16	230		(310)	
Translation adjustment for the period					4,483
Balances at October 31, 1986	49,545	1,070,845	(160,022)	(6,736)	(3,392)
Net earnings			26,592		
Cash dividends ($.10 per share)			(7,927)		
Exercise of stock options, net	105	2,260			
Amortization of executive stock plan expense				1,928	
Repurchase of restricted stock, net	(20)	(563)		441	
Repurchase of common stock	(293)	(5,528)			
Translation adjustment for the period					2,730
Quasi-Reorganization Revaluation adjustments, net		(438,222)			
Transfer to additional capital		(141,357)	141,357		
Balances at October 31, 1987	$49,337	$ 487,435	$ 0	$ (4,367)	$ (662)

Notes to Consolidated Financial Statements

Major Accounting Policies

Balance Sheet Revaluation. The balance sheet at October 31, 1987, has been adjusted to fair value in accordance with accounting principles applicable to quasi-reorganizations. See Restructuring Activities.

● ● ● ●

Restructuring Activities

Quasi-Reorganization. In conjunction with the company's restructuring and refocus on its engineering and construction business, the company, with the approval of the Board of Directors, adjusted its October 31, 1987, balance sheet to fair value and transferred the accumulated deficit of $141 million to Additional Capital in accordance with quasi-reorganization accounting principles. Management utilized the services of outside experts in conducting the revaluation. The principal adjustments to fair value included a $267 million reduction in the carrying value of the company's 57.5% interest in Doe Run; reversal of $62 million of deferred gains on sale leaseback transactions; accrual of $125 million for certain lease costs; revaluation of intangibles resulting in the elimination of $151 million of excess of cost over net assets of acquired businesses; recognition of a $22 million net increase in the value of the company's investment in Massey Coal Company; and $21 million net increase in the value of other assets. Management has given consideration to the carrying values of the company's remaining assets and liabilities and believes they approximate fair value. The fair value adjustments to the balance sheet resulted in a net charge to Additional Capital of $438 million.

• • • •

MARINE TRANSPORT LINES, INC. AND SUBSIDIARIES

Consolidated Balance Sheets
(in thousands except shares and per share data)

	December 31	
	1985	1984
Shareholders' equity—Notes D, E, G and L:		
• • • •		
Common Stock, par value $.10 per share: Authorized—6,000,000 shares. Issued and outstanding—1985, 3,010,775 shares; 1984, 2,388,775 shares	301	239
Additional capital	31,405	25,699
Foreign currency translation adjustment	117	
Retained earnings (after elimination of deficit of $28,933) since April 1, 1983	14,830	10,142
Total shareholders' equity	46,653	36,080

Consolidated Statements of Changes in Shareholders' Equity
(in thousands)

	Common Stock	Additional Capital	Foreign Currency Translation Adjustment	Retained Earnings (Deficit)	Retained Earnings Since April 1, 1983
Balance at December 31, 1982		$51,304		$(24,385)	
Effects of spin-off from GATX—Note D	$238	25,629			
Effects of quasi-reorganization —Note E		(51,253)		28,933	
Pro forma balance at December 31, 1982	238	25,680		4,548	
Net income—year ended December 31, 1983				(4,548)	$ 7,271
Balance at December 31, 1983	238	25,680			7,271
Common Stock issued under the Incentive Stock Option Plan, less unearned compensation —Note L	1	19			
Net income—year ended December 31, 1984					2,871
Balance at December 31, 1984	239	25,699			10,142
Value assigned to the warrants issued to GATX—Note G		1,125			
Common Stock issued in exchange for capital stock of IOBT —Note C	60	4,444			
Common Stock issued under the Incentive Stock Option Plan, less unearned compensation —Note L	2	137			

Consolidated Statements of Changes in Shareholders' Equity (continued)
(in thousands)

	Common Stock	Additional Capital	Foreign Currency Translation Adjustment	Retained Earnings (Deficit)	Retained Earnings Since April 1, 1983
Foreign currency gain on the translation of the Rowbotham balance sheet—Note A			$117		
Net income—year ended December 31, 1985					4,688
Balance at December 31, 1985	$301	$31,405	$117		$14,830

See notes to consolidated financial statements.

Notes to Consolidated Financial Statements

Note E. Quasi-Reorganization

Effective April 1, 1983, the Board of Directors of MTL authorized a restatement of MTL's balance sheet in accordance with accounting principles applicable to a quasi-reorganization. The Board's action resulted from a lengthy review of MTL's business, assets and strategy for future operations as a newly independent company.

The adjustments relating to the quasi-reorganization were as follows:

1. A write-off of the goodwill of $10,422,000 against additional capital;
2. A restatement of the net carrying amount of vessels to their estimated realizable values, including a reversal of a related reserve for vessel overhaul costs no longer required, by a charge of $11,898,000 against additional capital; and
3. The elimination of the $28,933,000 retained earnings deficit by reducing additional capital by a corresponding amount.

The write-off of goodwill was based on the Board's conclusion that it had no continuing value to MTL and its planned operations. The determination of the realizable values of vessels was based on a management review and subsequent transactions. Management gave consideration to the carrying amounts of MTL's remaining assets and liabilities and believed them to be fairly stated.

• • • •

MIDLAND SOUTHWEST CORPORATION AND SUBSIDIARIES

Consolidated Balance Sheets
December 31, 1986 and 1985

	1986	1985
Stockholders' Equity:		
Cumulative convertible preferred stock, par value $1.00; authorized 10,000,000 shares (Note 6):		
10% Series A, issued 1,000,000 shares in 1985		1,000
10% Series B, issued 986,000 shares in 1985		986
Common stock, no par value; authorized 500,000,000 shares; issued 224,370,000 shares in 1986; 4,775,000 shares in 1985	10,227	4,775
Additional paid-in capital	30,811	37,785
Accumulated deficit, prior to quasi-reorganization		(39,750)
Accumulated deficit, since January 6, 1986, net of $39,750,000 eliminated in quasi-reorganization	(15,926)	
	25,112	4,796
Less treasury stock, at cost, 83,000 shares in 1985		1,194
Total stockholders' equity	25,112	3,602

	1986	1985	1984
Series A Preferred Stock			
Beginning of year	$ 1,000	$ 1,000	
Issuance of 1,000,000 shares			$ 1,000
Exchange of preferred stock for common stock	(1,000)		
End of year		1,000	1,000
Series B Preferred Stock			
Beginning of year	986	307	
Issuance of 307,000 shares			307
Issuance of 679,000 shares		679	
Issuance of 3,547,000 shares	3,547		
Exchange of preferred stock for common stock	(4,533)		
End of year		986	307
Common Stock			
Beginning of year, 4,775,000 shares	4,775	4,775	4,775
Cancel 81,000 treasury shares	(81)		
Exchange of preferred stock for 219,676,000 shares of common	5,533		
End of year	10,227	4,775	4,775
Additional Paid-In Capital			
Beginning of year	37,785	31,676	11,943
Issuance of series A preferred			16,920
Issuance of series B preferred	31,921	6,118	2,758
Stock award transactions, net	(30)	(9)	55
Cancel treasury shares	(1,083)		
Quasi-Reorganization	(37,782)		
End of year	30,811	37,785	31,676
Accumulated Deficit			
Beginning of year, as reported	(37,782)	(19,995)	(9,106)
Cumulative effect of change in accounting method for oil and gas properties	(1,968)	(1,265)	(662)
Beginning of year, as restated	(39,750)	(21,260)	(9,768)
Quasi-Reorganization	39,750		
Net loss	(15,926)	(18,490)	(11,492)
End of year	(15,926)	(39,750)	(21,260)
Treasury Stock			
Beginning of year	(1,194)	(1,197)	(1,110)
Stock award transactions, net	30	3	(87)
Cancel treasury shares	(1,164)		
End of year		(1,194)	(1,197)
Shares, end of year		(83)	(83)
Deferred Compensation			
Beginning of year		(29)	(91)
Stock award transactions, net		29	62
End of year			(29)

See accompanying notes to consolidated financial statements.

Notes to Consolidated Financial Statements

• • • •

2. Long-Term Debt and Quasi-Reorganization

On September 26, 1985, the M.A. Hanna Company (Hanna), then owner of 49.9% of the Company's common stock outstanding and 100% of the Company's Series A and Series B convertible preferred stock outstanding, purchased the Company's long-term note payable from the banks and, accordingly, succeeded to the banks' rights under the loan agreement dated March 30, 1984. On January 6, 1986, Hanna agreed to exchange the note, in the principal amount of $29,045,000 plus accrued interest of $50,000 for 2,909,500 shares of the Company's Series B convertible preferred stock. With the debt exchange completed, and after consultation with legal counsel and review of applicable accounting and statutory regulations, management recommended and the Board of Directors approved an accounting quasi-reorganization to more accurately reflect the recorded values of assets, liabilities and stockholders' equity. The quasi-reorganization was effective January 6, 1986, and consisted of the following adjustments:

1) Fixed asset carrying values were adjusted to the Company's determination of fair market value. Accumulated depreciation was eliminated against the respective asset accounts and appropriate remaining lives and depreciation methods were selected for the adjusted basis of the assets. The only assets requiring carrying value adjustments were oil and gas properties, which were written up to the value of estimated future net cash flows based on prices prevailing on January 6, 1986, discounted at 10% per year. This adjustment amounted to $1,968,000. The Company's deep drilling equipment had previously been written down as discussed in Note 4 and required no further adjustment in the quasi-reorganization.

2) Accumulated deficit was eliminated against additional paid-in capital. The new retained earnings (or accumulated deficit) account will include the date January 6, 1986 in its title.

3) Treasury stock was cancelled, after the issuance of one remaining stock award commitment, with common stock reduced by the original $1.00 per share value and the balance applied against additional paid-in capital.

The following schedule shows the effects of the above transactions on stockholders' equity:

	December 31, 1985	Debt Exchange	Quasi-Reorganization	January 6, 1986
Series A preferred stock	$ 1,000,000			1,000,000
Series B preferred stock	986,000	2,905,000		3,891,000
Common stock	4,775,000		(81,000)	4,694,000
Additional paid-in capital	37,785,000	26,140,000	(38,895,000)	25,030,000
Accumulated deficit	(39,750,000)		39,750,000	
Treasury stock	(1,194,000)		1,194,000	
Total stockholders' equity	$ 3,602,000	29,045,000	1,968,000	34,615,000

4) Write-down of Assets

During 1985, the Company determined that the market for its deep drilling equipment had softened to the point that the carrying value of this equipment had become permanently impaired. The Company concluded that there was no probable expectation of realizing the existing carrying value through future operations and, accordingly, recorded a charge of $11,162,000 to reduce the net book value to an amount considered realizable in future periods.

During 1986, the oil and gas industry witnessed an unprecedented decline in oil and gas prices, which resulted in significant reductions in exploration and development activity. This decline appears to be long-term in nature, resulting from a fundamental weakness in the supply and demand equilibrium. Accordingly, the Company reviewed the carrying value of all assets and determined that the values assigned in the quasi-reorganization to its oil and gas properties and deep drilling equipment could not be reasonably expected to be recovered from future operations and were, therefore, permanently impaired. Accordingly, the Company recorded a charge to write down oil and gas properties by $3,500,000 and deep drilling equipment by $8,437,000.

• • • •

PUBLICKER INDUSTRIES, INC. AND SUBSIDIARY COMPANIES

Consolidated Balance Sheets at December 31, 1984 and 1983

	1984	1983
	(in thousands)	
Shareholders' equity (Notes 2 and 7):		
Common shares, 1984—$.10 par value, 1983—$5 par value. Authorized—20,000,000 shares; issued 1984—9,254,779 shares, 1983—8,816,464 shares	925	44,082
Additional paid-in capital	25,684	27,005
Accumulated deficit		(18,006)
Accumulated deficit (January 1, 1984)	(14,927)	
Cumulative translation adjustments (Notes 2 and 4)		(12,671)
Deferred employee compensation		(36)
Common shares held in treasury, at cost—443,837 shares	(3,828)	(3,828)
Total shareholders' equity	7,854	36,546

Consolidated Statements of Shareholders' Equity
for the Years Ended December 31, 1984, 1983, and 1982
(in thousands) (Notes 2, 6 and 7)

	Common Shares	Additional Paid-In Capital	Accumulated Deficit	Cumulative Translation Adjustments	Common Treasury Shares[1]	Deferred Employee Compensation
Balance December 31, 1981	$44,082	$27,291	$(12,071)	$(5,730)	$(3,825)	$(321)
Dividends—preferred		(140)				
Amortization of deferred employee compensation						143
Cancellation of deferred employee compensation		(9)			(2)	11
Translation adjustments 1982				(4,349)		
Net loss			(2,013)			
Balance December 31, 1982	44,082	27,142	(14,084)	(10,079)	(3,827)	(167)
Dividends—preferred		(139)				
Amortization of deferred employee compensation						132
Cancellation of deferred employee compensation		2			(1)	(1)
Translation adjustments—1983				(2,592)		
Net loss			(3,922)			
Balance December 31, 1983	44,082	27,005	(18,006)	(12,671)	(3,828)	(36)
Reclassification of par value (Note 7)	(43,200)	43,200				
Charges in connection with corporate revaluation (Note 2)			(27,905)	12,671		

Consolidated Statements of Shareholders' Equity (continued)
for the Years Ended December 31, 1984, 1983, and 1982
(in thousands) (Notes 2, 6 and 7)

	Common Shares	Additional Paid-In Capital	Accumulated Deficit	Cumulative Translation Adjustments	Common Treasury Shares[1]	Deferred Employee Compensation
Elimination of deficit by corporate revaluation at January 1, 1984 (Note 2)		(45,911)	45,911			
Balance January 1, 1984 as restated	882	24,294			(3,828)	(36)
Dividends—preferred		(139)				
Amortization of deferred employee compensation						36
Shares issued for contribution to pension plan	43	1,529				
Translation adjustments 1984				(5,375)		
Write-off of 1984 translation adjustments (Note 4)				5,375		
Net loss			(14,927)			
Balance December 31, 1984	$ 925	$25,684	$(14,927)	$ 0	$(3,828)	$ 0

[1]Represents 443,562; 443,712; 443,837; and 443,837 common shares held in Treasury at December 31, 1981, 1982, 1983 and 1984, respectively.

Notes to Consolidated Financial Statements

• • • •

Note 2. Corporate Revaluation

Effective January 1, 1984, the Company implemented a corporate revaluation. This revaluation permitted the Company to eliminate the adjusted accumulated deficit account as of that date, by a charge against additional paid-in capital, and to establish a new retained earnings account for the accumulation of the results of future operations.

In connection with the revaluation, management evaluated all of the Company's assets. As part of its asset redeployment strategy, the Company previously evaluated various alternatives regarding the industrial alcohol facility in Philadelphia, which had been idle since the first quarter of 1982. Since that time, market conditions have not improved and viable alternatives have not been developed. As a result, these assets, including those of the bulk liquid storage business, were revalued and adjusted on an estimated recoverable basis as of January 1, 1984. The revaluation included a provision of $9,524,000 for disposition of, and pension costs relating to, the Philadelphia facility.

The Company evaluated its other businesses, including its United Kingdom Beverage Division, as going concerns; the related assets were revalued and adjusted on a going-concern basis, after giving consideration to recent appraisals. (Subsequently, in March 1985, the Company adopted a plan to sell its U.K. Beverage Division and has further adjusted the carrying value of the related net assets [see Note 3].) The revaluation resulted in a charge to the accumulated deficit account as of January 1, 1984, of $27,905,000. This amount included the net write-down of assets, amounting to $5,710,000; the reversal of the Company's cumulative translation adjustment account of $12,671,000; and the provision for disposition and pension costs noted above.

The following is a summary of the change in the net assets of idle facilities referred to above during 1984 (in thousands):

	Estimated Recoverable Value of Idle Assets	Disposition, Carrying and Pension Cost Reserves	Net
Balance January 1, 1984, after Corporate Revaluation	$9,284	$(9,524)	$ (240)
1984 Activity	(634)	1,940	1,306
Balance December 31, 1984	$8,650	$(7,584)	$ 1,066

• • • •

STERLING ELECTRONICS CORPORATION

Consolidated Statements of Financial Position

	March 31, 1984	April 2, 1983
SHAREHOLDERS' EQUITY		
Cumulative convertible preferred stock, authorized 2,000,000 shares: Series A and B ($2.50 par value) —none issued; $.75 Series C, ($2.50 par value)— 29,590 shares issued (liquidation preference of $20 per share, aggregating $591,800) (Note 4)	73	73
....Common stock, $.50 par value: authorized 9,000,000 shares, issued 4,098,827 shares in 1983 and 1984 (Notes 4 and 8)	2,049	2,049
Additional paid-in capital (Note 5)	5,197	4,443
Earned surplus (deficit) from April 4, 1982 (Note 5)	164	(435)
	7,485	6,132
Less-Treasury stock....	780	944
	6,705	5,187

Consolidated Statements of Shareholders' Equity
Years Ended March 31, 1984, April 2, 1983, and April 3, 1982
(Notes 1, 4 and 8)

	Common Stock	Additional Paid-In Capital	Retained Earnings	Treasury Stock
BALANCE, March 28, 1981	$2,049	$8,762	$(4,304)	$944
Dividends on cumulative convertible preferred stock			(22)	
Net Loss			(683)	
Corporate Readjustment (Note 5)				
Elimination of accumulated deficit as of April 3, 1982		(5,009)	5,009	
Revaluation of property		690		
BALANCE, April 3, 1982	2,049	4,442		944
Acquisition of minority interest at less than book value		1		
Dividends on cumulative convertible preferred stock			(22)	
Net Loss			(412)	

Consolidated Statements of Shareholders' Equity (continued)
Years Ended March 31, 1984, April 2, 1983, and April 3, 1982
(Notes 1, 4 and 8)

	Common Stock	Additional Paid-In Capital	Retained Earnings	Treasury Stock
BALANCE, April 2, 1983	2,049	4,443	(435)	944
Acquisition of minority interest at less than book value		2		
Dividend on cumulative convertible preferred stock			(22)	
Gain realized on sale of property in excess of revaluation of April 3, 1982 net of minority interest (Note 5)		204		
Sale of 82,000 shares held by Sterling Computer Systems				(164)
Federal Income Tax Credit (Note 2)		546		
Net Income			621	
BALANCE, March 31, 1984	$2,049	$5,197	$ 164	$780

Notes to Consolidated Financial Statements
March 31, 1984, April 2, 1983 and April 3, 1982

• • • •

5. Corporate Readjustment

On February 3, 1982, by action of the Board of Directors (Nevada requires no shareholder consent), the accumulated deficit at April 3, 1982, was eliminated by a charge to additional paid-in capital. The amount of this charge was $5,009,555. Subsequent to this action, consideration was given to the carrying value of the Company's assets and it was determined that the value of real property used by Phaostron Instruments for its manufacturing facility in South Pasadena, California should be revalued to estimated net realizable market value; other assets appeared to be fairly stated at that time. The revaluation of real property increased Sterling shareholders' equity $690,045 through a credit to additional paid-in capital. This property was sold for cash in August 1983. Gross selling price was $1,225,000. Net cash proceeds after retiring the mortgage on the property and costs of the sale was $1,029,500. Gain on the sale in excess of realization of the 1982 revaluation was $222,811 of which $204,541 was added to the Additional Paid-In Capital of shareholders' equity. The minority interests of Phaostron Instruments received credit for $18,270.

• • • •

THE UNION METAL MANUFACTURING COMPANY AND SUBSIDIARIES

Consolidated Balance Sheets

	December 31	
	1983	1982
Shareholders' equity		
Common shares with a par value of $1.00 a share: Authorized 2,400,000 shares; Issued (including shares held in treasury) 1983—1,050,144; 1982—1,047,644	1,050	1,047
Other capital	6,374	10,890
Retained earnings		12,148
	7,424	24,086
Less cost of common shares in treasury	148	
Total shareholders' equity	7,275	24,086

Statements of Consolidated Shareholders' Equity
Years Ended December 31, 1981, 1982, and 1983

	Common Shares	Other Capital	Treasury Shares	Retained Earnings	Total
Year ended December 31, 1981					
Balance at January 1, 1981—as previously reported	$ 887	$ 8,275		$12,499	$21,662
Cumulative restatement adjustment —Note C				2,473	2,473
Balance at January 1, 1981 —as restated	887	8,275		14,973	24,136
Net income				1,639	1,639
Shares issued in connection with:					
Acquisition	60	922			982
Employment		13			13
10% stock dividend paid:					
Shares	94	1,638		(1,733)	
Cash in lieu of fractional shares				(8)	(8)
Cash dividends paid —$.29 per share				(303)	(303)
Balance at December 31, 1981 —as restated	1,042	10,850		14,567	26,460
Year ended December 31, 1982					
Net loss				(2,315)	(2,315)
Shares issued in connection with:					
Employment	5	40			45
Cash dividends paid —$.10 per share				(104)	(104)
Balance at December 31, 1982 —as restated	1,047	10,890		12,148	24,086
Year ended December 31, 1983					
Net loss				(17,316)	(17,316)
Treasury shares:					
Purchased			(103)		(103)
Forfeiture of shares issued in connection with employment agreement			(45)		(45)
Shares issued in connection with Employment	2	21			23
Cash dividends paid —$.05 per share				(52)	(52)
Corporate readjustment:					
Elimination of accumulated deficit as of December 31, 1983		(5,220)		5,220	
Revaluation of property		683			683
Balance at December 31, 1983	$1,050	$ 6,374	$(148)	$ 0	$ 7,275

( ) Indicates deduction.

Notes to Consolidated Financial Statements
December 31, 1983

Note A. Summary of Significant Accounting Policies

Principles of Consolidation.

• • • •

The 1983 financial statements reflect the adjustments resulting from a corporate readjustment effected in the form of a quasi-reorganization as of December 31, 1983 (see Note B).

• • • •

Property, Plant, and Equipment. Property, plant, and equipment is stated at estimated fair value at December 31, 1983 (see Note B), and on the basis of cost at December 31, 1982. Plant and equipment are depreciated by the straight-line method over the estimated useful lives of the assets.

Note B. Corporate Readjustment

By action of the Board of Directors (Ohio requires no shareholder consent), the accumulated retained-earnings deficit at December 31, 1983, was eliminated by a charge of $5,220,720 to other capital. Additionally, the carrying values of real property, machinery and equipment used at the Hampton, Virginia, and Frankfort, Indiana, facilities as well as at the Apple Creek, Ohio, and the continuing Canton, Ohio, facilities were increased to their estimated fair values; other assets approximate estimated fair values. The effect of this revaluation was to increase both property, plant and equipment and other capital by $683,424.

● ● ● ●

UNDER BANKRUPTCY PROCEEDING

CONTINENTAL MORTGAGE INVESTORS

Consolidated Balance Sheet
March 31, 1985 and 1984
(in thousands except share and per-share amounts)

	1985	1984
Shareholders' equity:		
Preferred shares, par value $1. Authorized 32,000,000 shares. Issued and outstanding 32,000,000 shares	32,000	32,000
Common shares, par value $.001. Authorized 50,000,000 shares. Issued and outstanding 21,400,000 shares	21	21
Paid-in capital	13,179	14,139
Deficit—subsequent to reorganization at March 31, 1983	(2,279)	(1,551)
Total shareholders' equity	42,921	44,609

Consolidated Statement of Shareholders' Equity
for the Years Ended March 31, 1985, 1984, and 1983
(in thousands)

	Preferred Shares	Common Shares	Shares of Beneficial Interest (Cancelled 3/31/83)	Paid-In Capital	Retained Earnings (Deficit)
Balance April 1, 1982			$146,658		$(167,906)
Net loss					(21,565)
Bankruptcy reorganization transactions:					
Cancellation of shares of beneficial interest			(146,658)	$146,658	
Issuance of common shares		$21		17,979	
Issuance of preferred shares	$32,000				
Reorganization accounting adjustments:					
Revaluation of assets:					
Real estate under development				16,945	
Goodwill				25,489	
Other				379	
Elimination of deficit				(189,471)	189,471

Consolidated Statement of Shareholders' Equity (continued)
for the Years Ended March 31, 1985, 1984, and 1983
(in thousands)

	Preferred Shares	Common Shares	Shares of Beneficial Interest (Cancelled 3/31/83)	Paid-In Capital	Retained Earnings (Deficit)
Balance March 31, 1983	32,000	21		17,979	
Net loss					(1,551)
Cash dividends paid on Preferred shares				(3,840)	
Balance March 31, 1984	32,000	21		14,139	(1,551)
Net loss					(728)
Cash dividend paid on Preferred shares				(960)	
Balance March 31, 1985	$32,000	$21	$ 0	$ 13,179	$ (2,279)

Notes to Consolidated Financial Statements
(in thousands except share and per-share amounts)

1. Bankruptcy Proceedings and Reorganization

On March 8, 1976, Continental Mortgage Investors ("Continental" or the "Company") filed a petition under Chapter XI of the Federal Bankruptcy Act. The case was ordered transferred to proceedings for the reorganization of a corporation under Chapter X of the Bankruptcy Act by the United States District Court, District of Massachusetts (the "Court") on May 1, 1979. During Chapter X proceedings, a Court-appointed Trustee managed Continental's property and conducted its business.

● ● ● ●

3. Reorganization Accounting

Because of the Company's reorganization under the bankruptcy laws and its substantial change in capitalization as described in Note 1, the Company specified a new basis of accounting for its assets and liabilities under reorganization principles of accounting at March 31, 1983. Under such principles, assets are revalued to their estimated fair values, liabilities are recorded at discounted present values to amounts expected to be paid and the prior deficit in retained earnings is eliminated against paid-in capital.

In accordance with the above, the Company revalued the Hawaii Loa Ridge property to $36,250, which represented its estimated fair value, net of the tax effect of the difference between the tax basis and book basis of the assets. Of this amount, $750 represented the fair value of a sales center which was classified in property and equipment. Mortgage notes receivable, which previously had been carried at discounted amounts to reflect the difference between the market rates at the time of the financing and the stated rate of 13%, were revalued to their face amount to reflect current market rates. All other assets and liabilities were stated at their then current book amounts. The excess of the aggregate consideration (cash and securities) distributed as part of the bankruptcy reorganization over the restated value of the net tangible assets was reflected on the books as goodwill.

As a result of the reorganization accounting, a deficit in retained earnings totaling $189,471 at March 31, 1983, was eliminated against paid-in capital.

● ● ● ●

CRYSTAL OIL COMPANY AND SUBSIDIARIES

Consolidated Balance Sheets

	December 31	
	1986	1985
	(in thousands)	

STOCKHOLDERS' EQUITY (DEFICIENCY)
Preferred stock, $.01 par value; authorized 150,000,000 shares:
$.06 senior convertible voting preferred stock (non-cumulative): $1.00 liquidation preference; 50,062,000 shares issued 501

Consolidated Balance Sheets (continued)

	December 31	
	1986	1985
	(in thousands)	
Series A convertible voting preferred stock: $1.00 liquidation preference; 66,867,000 shares issued	669	
Common stock, $.01 par value; authorized 2,300,000,000 and 90,000,000 shares; issued 123,447,723 and 51,505,723 shares, respectively	1,204	515
Additional paid-in capital	10,348	68,406
Accumulated deficit		(100,084)
TOTAL STOCKHOLDERS' EQUITY (DEFICIENCY)	12,722	(31,163)

Consolidated Statements of Stockholders' Equity (Deficiency)

	Senior Preferred Stock	Series A Preferred Stock	Common Stock	Additional Paid-In Capital	Accumulated Deficit
			(in thousands)		
Balance at January 1, 1984			$20,937	$30,921	$ (10,896)
Net loss					(21,357)
Cash dividends on common stock				(5,653)	
Balance at December 31, 1984			20,937	25,268	(32,253)
Net loss					(67,831)
Issuance of $1 par value common stock in exchange offers			7,418	2,782	
Conversion of $1 par value to $.01			(28,072)	28,072	
Issuance of $.01 par value common stock for payment of obligations			232	12,284	
Balance at December 31, 1985			515	68,406	(100,084)
Net loss					(232,182)
Issuance of $.01 par value common stock for payment of obligations			2	48	
Issuance of preferred and common stock	$501	$669	1,204		
Retirement of existing common stock			(517)		
Net adjustment relating to restatement of assets and liabilities				(58,106)	332,266
Balance at December 31, 1986	$501	$669	$ 1,204	$10,348	

Notes to Consolidated Financial Statements
December 31, 1986

Note A. Significant Accounting Policies

• • • •

Basis of Presentation. On October 1, 1986, Crystal Oil Company ("Crystal") filed a petition for reorganization under Chapter 11 of the United States Bankruptcy Code (the "Bankruptcy Code") in the United States Bankruptcy Court for the Western District of Louisiana, Shreveport Division (the "Court"). On December 31, 1986, the Court entered an order confirming the Second Amended and Restated Plan of Reorganization (the "Plan") of Crystal which became effective on January 30, 1987. The terms of the Plan are summarized in Note B.

The Company has accounted for the reorganization as a quasi-reorganization. Accordingly, all assets and liabilities have been restated to reflect their estimated fair value as of December 31, 1986. This restatement resulted in a net credit of $274.2 million, which was applied first to eliminate the accumulated deficit at December 31, 1986, of $332.3 million and the difference was recorded as a charge against additional paid-in capital.

Crude Oil and Natural Gas Properties.

• • • •

In connection with the implementation of Crystal's Plan, crude oil and natural gas properties were restated to reflect their estimated fair value at December 31, 1986, as determined by an independent petroleum engineering firm.

Note B. Emergence From Chapter 11 Bankruptcy Proceedings

As discussed in Note A, Crystal filed a petition for reorganization under Chapter 11 of the Bankruptcy Code on October 1, 1986. On December 31, 1986, the Court confirmed the Plan, which became effective on January 30, 1987.

• • • •

The Company has accounted for the reorganization as a quasi-reorganization. Accordingly, all assets and liabilities were recorded at their estimated fair value. The following table summarizes the adjustments required to record the accounting reorganization and the issuance of the various securities in connection with implementation of the Plan.

	Historical Balance December 31, 1986	Reorganization Adjustments Debit	Reorganization Adjustments Credit	Restated Balance December 31, 1986
		(in thousands)		
ASSETS				
Current assets:				
Cash	$ 10,959			$ 10,959
Accounts receivable	8,174		228[1]	7,946
Prepaid expenses and other	2,030		1,000[2]	1,030
Total property, plant, and equipment	89,428		10,213[3]	79,215
Other assets	2,838		61[3]	2,777
TOTAL ASSETS	$113,429		$ 11,502	$101,927
LIABILITIES AND STOCKHOLDERS' EQUITY				
Current liabilities:				
Accounts payable and accrued expenses	$ 38,314	$ 27,449[4]	$ 3,756[5]	$ 14,621
Current portion of long-term obligations	338,410	322,204[1]		16,206
Long-term obligations			58,378[6]	58,378
Stockholder's equity:				
Senior preferred stock			501[7]	501
Series A preferred stock			669[7]	669
Common stock	517	517[7]	1,204[7]	1,204
Additional paid-in capital	68,454	58,106[7]		10,348
Accumulated deficit	(332,266)		332,266[7]	
TOTAL LIABILITIES AND STOCKHOLDERS' EQUITY	$113,429	$408,276	$396,774	$101,927

[1]The adjustment to accounts receivable consists primarily of offsetting miscellaneous receivable balances against corresponding current liability balances. *(continued)*

²During 1986, the Company prepaid certain legal fees in connection with its reorganization. This adjustment applies the prepaid balance against the corresponding accrued liability for reorganization costs.

³The adjustments to property, plant, and equipment and other assets are recorded to restate the assets to their estimated fair value. The determination of the fair values is based primarily upon evaluations and studies by an independent petroleum engineering firm, other independent experts, and management and takes into account current market conditions in the crude oil and natural gas industry.

⁴The reduction in accounts payable and accrued expenses is primarily attributable to (a) the elimination of approximately $18.8 million of interest accrued on unsecured debt which the Company will not be required to pay according to the provisions of the Plan; (b) the reclassification of approximately $6.7 million of other obligations to long-term due to extended repayment terms; and (c) the elimination of approximately $2.0 million in other obligations which the Company does not expect to pay pursuant to Federal Bankruptcy Law.

⁵The increase in accounts payable and accrued expenses is primarily attributable to the accrual of the estimated reorganization costs including legal fees, investment advisor fees, other professional and administrative expenses associated with the reorganization, and the adjustments described in 1. and 2. above.

⁶The adjustments to current portion of long-term obligations and long-term obligations are primarily attributable to (a) a decrease of $290.6 million to current portion of long-term obligations to eliminate the carrying value of the Company's senior subordinated secured notes and its subordinated unsecured debt according to provisions of the Plan; (b) a decrease of $31.5 million to current portion of long-term obligations with a corresponding increase to long-term obligations to reclassify the Company's senior secured debt based on the terms of the new loan agreements; (c) an increase of $19.7 million to long-term obligations to record the issuance of the non-interest bearing convertible subordinated secured notes due 1997 according to the provisions of the Plan; and (d) a reclassification of other obligations described in 4. above.

⁷The adjustments to stockholders' equity represent (a) the issuance of the various equity securities in connection with the implementation of the Plan; (b) the retirement of the Company's previously issued Common Stock; (c) the elimination of the accumulated deficit as of the date of the reorganization; and (d) the charge against additional paid-in capital for the net effect of all reorganization entries.

• • • •

MESTEK, INC.

Consolidated Balance Sheet

	December 31		October 31,
	1985	1984	1984
Common Shareholders' Equity:			
Common Stock—1,791,110 shares issued	89	89	89
Additional Paid-In Capital	980	598	598
Retained Earnings after eliminating accumulated deficit of $60,935,338 at October 31, 1984	141		
	1,212	688	688
Less:			
Treasury Shares, at cost—48,329, 49,214 and 49,208 shares	(346)	(362)	(362)
Total Common Shareholders' Equity	865	325	325

Consolidated Statement of Changes in Common Shareholders' Equity
for the Two Months Ended December 31, 1984 and
for the Year Ended December 31, 1985

	Common Stock	Paid-In Capital	Retained Earnings	Treasury Shares	Total
Balance October 31, 1984	$89	$598		$(362)	$325
Net income			$ 37		37
Amortization of excess redemption value of Redeemable Preferred Stock over fair value			(36)		(36)
Balance December 31, 1984	$89	$598		$(362)	$325
Net income			295		295
Tax Effect of Operating Loss Carryforward		333			333
Amortization of excess redemption value of Redeemable Preferred Stock over fair value			(157)		(157)
Distribution of Treasury Shares in settlement of pre-reorganization claim		(3)	(13)	16	
Adjustment of pre-reorganization liabilities to employees		39			39
Other—net		12	15		28
Balance December 31, 1985	$89	$980	$141	$(346)	$865

Notes to the Consolidated Financial Statements

Note 1. Accounting Policies

Basis of Presentation. During the period from December 31, 1981, and October 31, 1984, Mestek, Inc. (formerly Mesta Machine Company, the "Company") implemented a plan of reorganization as is described in Note 3. Significant events which occurred during the reorganization included the discontinuance of manufacturing operations, the sale of assets by the Company and certain of its subsidiaries, and the settlement of liabilities during the bankruptcy proceedings. Due to the significance of the changes to the Company during this period, a comparison of current financial data with pre-reorganization data would not be meaningful. In order to show its current financial position the Company has included balance sheets as of December 31, 1985 and 1984, and October 31, 1984. The Company has also presented statements of income, changes in financial position and changes in shareholders' equity for the year ended December 31, 1985 and the two months ended December 31, 1984. These financial statements present the operations of the Company subsequent to the implementation of the plan of reorganization.

In order to show the financial effects of the reorganization, the Company has presented the unaudited Reconciliation of Balance Sheets from December 31, 1981, to October 31, 1984. The Company believes that this presentation is more beneficial to the readers' understanding of the reorganization than the inclusion of full financial statements for that period.

The Company has accounted for the reorganization in a manner similar to a quasi-reorganization. The extinguishment of liabilities, restatement and distribution of assets and issuance of debt and equity securities to former creditors pursuant to the plan of reorganization resulted in a net credit of $61,533,927. This credit was applied first to eliminate the retained deficit at October 31, 1984, and the remainder was recorded as additional paid-in capital.

• • • •

Note 3. Reorganization Proceedings (Unaudited)

On February 9, 1983, the Company filed a petition for reorganization under Chapter 11 of the United States Bankruptcy Code. On March 28, 1984, the Company filed with the United States Bankruptcy Court for the Western District of Pennsylvania (the "Bankruptcy Court") a proposed amended plan of reorganization (as revised, the "Mesta Plan"). The Mesta Plan was approved by vote of the creditors, former employees, retirees and shareholders of the Company, and on June 25, 1984, the

Bankruptcy Court entered an order confirming the Mesta Plan. This confirmation order was approved by the United States District Court for the Western District of Pennsylvania (the "District Court") on June 26, 1984.

On October 19, 1984, the Company began its distribution of cash, stock and other securities to creditors, former employees and retirees as provided for in the Mesta Plan. As of October 31, 1984, substantially all of these distributions had been made (the period from October 19 through October 31, 1984, is hereinafter referred to as the "Distribution Period"). The Bankruptcy Court entered its final decree in the Company's bankruptcy proceedings on January 31, 1985. This final decree was approved by the District Court on February 20, 1985.

As part of its reorganization, the Company discontinued its primary line of business, which had been the manufacture of machinery and equipment for the metals industry. In connection with this, the Company sold its manufacturing plants, substantially all of its machinery and equipment and the assets of certain of its subsidiaries related to that line of business.

● ● ● ●

During its reorganization, the Company sold its manufacturing plants, substantially all of its machinery and equipment and the assets of certain of its subsidiaries which were involved in the manufacture of machinery and equipment for the metals industry. The amounts shown as decreases in accounts receivable, inventories, property, plant and equipment, other assets and accounts payable are the assets sold by the Company and liabilities assumed by the buyers. The cash increase represents the cash payments received by the Company, and the increase to retained earnings is the net gain realized on the sales. A net gain was realized at the time of the sales because the value of certain of the assets had previously been written down as part of the shut-down reserves. These write-downs are included in the Operations section.

● ● ● ●

The distributions to creditors, extinguishment of debt and general restructuring of assets and liabilities produced a net credit of $61,533,927. This credit was applied first to eliminate the retained deficit at October 31, 1984, and the remainder was recorded as paid-in capital. See Note 1 to the consolidated financial statements.

● ● ● ●

OXOCO, INC.

Consolidated Balance Sheets

	December 31	
	1985	1986
Stockholders' equity (deficit):		
Common stock, $0.10 par value, 20,000,000 shares authorized, 7,271,668 issued and outstanding at December 31, 1985	727	
Common stock, $0.01 par value, 12,500,000 shares authorized, 6,216,214 shares to be issued		62
Preferred stock, $1.00 par value, 5,000,000 shares authorized, 817,097 shares of $3.00 Cumulative Convertible Preferred Stock, issued and outstanding, liquidation value $25 per share, aggregating $20,427,425 at December 31, 1985	817	
● ● ● ●		
Additional capital	39,046	7,937
Accumulated deficit prior to December 31, 1986	(72,413)	
Retained earnings at December 31, 1986		
Total stockholders' equity (deficit)	(31,823)	8,000

Consolidated Statements of Stockholders' Equity (Deficit)

	$3.00 Cumulative Convertible Preferred Stock	Common Stock $0.10 Par	Common Stock $0.01 Par	Additional Capital	Retained Earnings (Accumulated Deficit)
Balances at January 1, 1984	$700	$691		$34,171	$13,232
Issuance in connection with acquisitions	117	35		4,875	
Valuation allowance					(2,302)
Preferred dividends					1,738
Net income					
Balance at December 31, 1984	817	727		39,046	12,668
Valuation allowance					(379)
Preferred dividends					(84,702)
Net loss					
Balance at December 31, 1985	817	727		39,046	(72,413)
Issuance in connection with financial advisor fees		147		202	
Confirmation of the plan of reorganization	(817)	(874)	58	8,792	
Conversion of plan payments			4	508	
Net income					31,802
Accumulated deficit offset				(40,611)	40,611
Balance at December 31, 1986	$ 0	$ 0	$62	$ 7,937	$ 0

Notes to Consolidated Financial Statements

• • • •

2. Reorganization and Asset Revaluation

• • • •

Asset Revaluation. Pursuant to the reorganization of the Company, net assets were revalued at December 31, 1986. Five venture capital funds managed by Hambrecht & Quist Venture Partners ("H&Q") reached agreements on December 30 and 31, 1986, and consummated such agreements in early 1987, with six holders of Class 4, 5 and 6 Claims, to acquire approximately 53% of the Company's New Common Stock issued pursuant to the Plan. Subsequent to the acquisition of these claims, H&Q exercised its option to request the Company to convert the Plan Payments into 400,000 shares of New Common Stock. H&Q valued the New Common Stock issuable under the Plan, assuming simultaneous conversion of Plan Payments to New Common Stock, at an immediate and unconditional price of $1.28 per share ($8,000,000). Further, the claim holders were given a choice to sell their holdings at a delayed and conditional price of $1.44 per share. The majority of claim holders (five of six) were paid $1.44 per share. The asset revaluation has been based on the unconditional price of $1.28 per share, which was also the share issue price for the subsequent capital infusion discussed in Note 13. The revaluation resulted in a downward adjustment of assets of $6,616,396, which is included in the summary of write-downs discussed in Note 4 and approximates the write-downs that would have occurred through revaluations based on fair market value.

As the Plan was confirmed prior to December 31, 1986, the effects of the debt extinguishment and reorganization were recorded in the 1986 consolidated financial statements and resulted in an extraordinary gain, which is summarized as follows:

Cancellation of subordinated debt	$85,862,674
Cancellation of accrued interest on subordinated debt	22,403,515
Write-off of deferred debt issue costs	(2,190,235)
Conversion of subordinated debt claims into New Common Stock and Additional Capital	(7,107,915)
Recognition of Class 3 Claims, net	(230,542)
Recognition of NCC Claim, net	(341,543)
Gain on extinguishment of 10.625% Installment Notes	342,879
Other	(81,671)
Extraordinary gain, gross and net of tax	$98,657,162

Accumulated deficit of $40,611,474 has been offset against additional capital pursuant to the reorganization, thereby eliminating accumulated deficit at December 31, 1986.

• • • •

4. Asset Write-Downs

Components of asset write-downs were as follows:

	Year Ended December 31		
	1984	1985	1986
Write-down of domestic full cost pool		$43,821,590	$30,958,472
Foreign cost center abandonments	677,163	4,680,652	2,718,853
Write-down of investment securities		4,539,126	
Write-down of natural gas pipelines		3,215,316	
Asset revaluations pursuant to reorganization			6,616,396
Totals	$677,163	$56,256,684	$40,293,721

• • • •

Pursuant to the reorganization of the Company, net assets were revalued at December 31, 1986. The asset revaluation was based on the unconditional price of $1.28 per share of New Common Stock discussed in Note 2, and reflects write-downs of oil and gas properties, natural gas pipelines, fee property and tubular goods and wellhead equipment, which approximate the write-downs that would have occurred through revaluations based on fair market value.

ASSETS AND LIABILITIES RESTATED

Some companies that have applied quasi-reorganizations and restated some or all assets have additionally restated liabilities at the time of the quasi-reorganization. Nine examples of such companies are presented below. The examples are classified according to whether or not the company was being reorganized in bankruptcy at the time of the quasi-reorganization.

NOT UNDER BANKRUPTCY PROCEEDING

ALAMCO, INC. AND SUBSIDIARIES

Consolidated Balance Sheet
December 31, 1985 and 1984
(in thousands)

	1985	1984
Stockholders' equity:		
• • • •		
Common stock, par value $1.00 per share; 25,000,000 shares authorized; 14,843,105 shares issued	14,843	14,843
Paid-in capital	140	20,921
Retained earnings		21,094
Retained earnings (since September 30, 1985) (Note 2)	442	
	15,425	56,858
Less treasury stock, 234,057 shares at lower of cost or net book value as of date of quasi-reorganization	234	876
Total stockholders' equity	15,191	55,982

Consolidated Statement of Stockholders' Equity
Years Ended December 31, 1985, 1984, and 1983
(in thousands)

	Common Stock	Paid-In Capital	Retained Earnings	Retained Since 9/30/85	Treasury Stock
Balance, December 31, 1984	14,843	20,921	21,094		876
Net income (loss)			(11,713)	$442	
Quasi-reorganization adjustments at September 30, 1985 (Note 2):					
Restatement of assets and liabilities to estimated value			(29,520)		
Adjustment of carrying value of treasury stock to net book value		(642)			(642)
Transfer of retained earnings deficit at September 30, 1985 to paid-in capital		(20,139)	20,139		
Balance, December 31, 1985	$14,843	$ 140	$ 0	$442	$234

Notes to Consolidated Financial Statements

1. Summary of Significant Accounting Policies

• • • •

Gas and Oil Producing Properties. Gas and oil producing properties are presented following the successful efforts method of accounting in accordance with rules defined by the Securities and Exchange Commission or estimated fair market value at September 30, 1985, the date of the quasi-reorganization (Note 2).

• • • •

Property, Plant and Equipment. Property, plant and equipment are stated at the lower of cost or estimated fair market value at September 30, 1985, the effective date of the quasi-reorganization (see Note 2).

• • • •

2. Quasi-Reorganization

The Company, with the approval of its Board of Directors, revalued its assets and liabilities to estimated fair values and implemented a quasi-reorganization effective September 30, 1985. The quasi-reorganization reflects management's judgment that the price of oil and natural gas will remain depressed for the foreseeable future, thereby impairing the Company's ability to fully recover its investment in both oil and gas properties and equipment used in the exploration and development of such properties. The effect of the adjustment to fair market value includes a reduction in the carrying value of oil and gas properties of approximately $24,350,000 net of accumulated depreciation, depletion and amortization, a reduction in fixed assets of approximately $3,816,000 net of accumulated depreciation, of approximately $3,600,000 in various accounts receivable the security for which is oil and gas reserves, and a reduction of $962,000 in the carrying value of certain investments and other assets. After a reduction in deferred taxes of approximately $3,208,000, the net effect of the adjustment of $29,520,000 was deducted from retained earnings, resulting in a deficit of $20,139,000. This deficit was then transferred to additional paid-in capital effective September 30, 1985. Additionally, the carrying value of treasury stock was adjusted to the net book value per share of common stock, giving effect to the quasi-reorganization. This action, which under Delaware law does not require stockholder approval, permits the Company to report undistributed earnings subsequent to September 30, 1985 as retained earnings, instead of as a reduction of the deficit transferred to additional paid-in capital.

• • • •

ALLIANCE WELL SERVICE, INC. AND SUBSIDIARIES

Consolidated Balance Sheet

	December 31	
	1983	1984
	(in thousands)	
Stockholders' Equity (Deficit):		
Common stock, $.01 par value—60,000,000 shares authorized; 2,633,532 and 15,039,334 shares issued in 1983 and 1984, respectively	26	150
Common stock warrants	22	35
Additional paid-in capital	11,490	17,609
Treasury stock, at cost (10,000 shares)	(17)	
Retained deficit	(12,676)	
Retained deficit, since elimination of deficit of $17,525,000 at September 30, 1984		(1,196)
Total Stockholders' Equity (Deficit)	(1,155)	16,598

Consolidated Statements of Stockholders' Equity (Deficit)
(in thousands)

	Common Stock	Common Stock Warrants	Additional Paid-In Capital	Treasury Stock	Retained Earnings (Deficit)
Balance December 31, 1981	$ 26	$22	$11,435		$ 4,499
Net loss					(6,156)
Shares issued to officer			61		
Return of Shares from officer				$(61)	
Balance December 31, 1982	26	22	11,496	(61)	(1,657)
Net loss					(11,019)
Shares issued in settlement of lawsuit			(6)	44	
Balance December 31, 1983	26	22	11,490	(17)	(12,676)
Net loss					(6,045)
Shares issued in private placement	50		4,952		
Shares issued in settlement of liabilities	3	35	185		
Shares issued in exchange for bank debt	26		3,136		
Shares issued to acquire Stanley	36		3,659		
Shares issued for exchange ratio difference	9				
Purchase of stock warrants		(22)	(80)		
Quasi-Reorganization			(5,716)		17,525
Cancellation of treasury stock				(17)	17
Balance December 31, 1984	$150	$35	$17,609	$ 0	$ (1,196)

Notes to Consolidated Financial Statements

Note 1. Basis of Accounting and Summary of Significant Accounting Policies

Alliance Well Service, Inc. (the Company) was incorporated in 1984 for the purpose of combining the operations of Monument Energy Services, Inc. (Monument) and Stanley Well Service, Inc. (Stanley). On March 8, 1984, Monument entered into a Joint Plan of Agreement and Reorganization with

Stanley in which Monument and Stanley would be merged and controlled by a new holding company (Alliance Well Service, Inc.). Consummation of the Agreement was conditional on several matters, including the successful placement of an equity interest in the Company for $5,000,000, a successful restructuring of the existing indebtedness with Monument's and Stanley's bank lenders, the approval of stockholders and other customary closing conditions. Such conditions were met and, as more fully described in Note 2, the merger became effective September 28, 1984, and was accounted for as a purchase of Stanley by Monument. Accordingly, under purchase accounting, the assets and liabilities of Stanley were recorded at their fair market value at the date of purchase. Also in connection with this transaction, Monument effected a quasi-reorganization whereby all of its assets and liabilities were revalued to their estimated fair market value and its retained earnings deficit was eliminated. These revaluations resulted in writedowns of Stanley's and Monument's net assets of $2,125,000 and $5,030,000, respectively.

• • • •

Going Concern Status. As shown in the consolidated financial statements, Monument incurred net losses of $6,156,000 and $11,019,000 during the years ended December 31, 1982 and 1983, respectively. As of December 31, 1983, Monument had a working capital deficit of $46,545,000 (including $42,706,000 of long-term bank debt classified as current) and a stockholders' deficit of $1,155,000. Also at December 31, 1983, Monument had failed to make mandatory prepayments of principal and scheduled payments of interest as required by its loan agreement and was not in compliance with certain financial covenants of such agreement. These factors, among others, indicated at December 31, 1983, that Monument's ability to continue as a going concern was dependent upon its ability to negotiate a restructured loan agreement, to obtain additional working capital and to reduce operating losses.

Note 2. Acquisition and Quasi-Reorganization

Effective September 28, 1984, the Company effected the mergers of Monument and Stanley into wholly owned subsidiaries of the Company. The mergers have been accounted for as a purchase of Stanley by Monument and, accordingly, the results of operations of Stanley have been included in the accompanying consolidated statements of loss since the effective date of the mergers.

– On September 30, 1984, the Company effected a quasi-reorganization of Monument whereby all of Monument's assets and liabilities were revalued to their estimated fair market value and its retained earnings deficit eliminated. The quasi-reorganization permits the Company to reflect the results of operations subsequent to September 30, 1984, separate from the retained earnings deficit that was eliminated against additional paid-in capital.

Unaudited information reflecting the Company's pro forma operating results from continuing operations assuming the acquisition had been consummated at the beginning of 1983 is not presented because pursuant to the Joint Plan of Agreement and Reorganization described in Note 1, the acquisition and quasi-reorganization are inseparable and such disclosure is not considered meaningful.

• • • •

Note 4. Long-Term Debt

• • • •

Prior to the execution of the new loan agreement, Monument restructured its existing indebtedness by converting $17,008,000 in principal and $7,100,000 of accrued interest into an aggregate of 2,529,208 shares of Monument common stock. After crediting common stock for the par value of the shares issued, the remaining gain was credited directly to additional paid-in capital, as opposed to income, because the debt restructuring coincided with the Company's quasi-reorganization.

• • • •

AMERICAN PACIFIC CORPORATION

Consolidated Balance Sheets

	September 30	
	1985	1984
Common Shareholders' equity		
Common Stock—$.10 par value, 12,000,000 shares authorized; issued and outstanding—3,268,948 and 6,221,281 shares in 1985 and 1984	327	622
Capital in excess of par value	8,320	59,660
Accumulated deficit		(29,495)
Total common shareholders' equity	8,647	30,787

Consolidated Statements of Shareholders' Equity

	Par Value of Shares Issued and Outstanding Common Stock	Capital in Excess of Par Value	Accumulated Deficit
Balance, September 30, 1984	622	59,660	(29,495)
Exchange of net assets of discontinued segment for common shares and retirement of such shares	(295)	(6,931)	
Net loss			(20,849)
Balance before quasi-reorganization	327	52,729	(50,344)
Quasi-Reorganization:			
Adjust net assets of continuing operations to fair value		5,935	
Eliminate accumulated deficit		(50,344)	50,344
Balance, September 30, 1985	$327	$ 8,320	$ 0

Notes to Consolidated Financial Statements

1. Summary of Significant Accounting Policies

Principles of Consolidation

• • • •

During fiscal 1985, the Company discontinued the operations of and disposed of the net assets of its residential real estate development and housing segment and disposed of the net assets of its financial services segment. In connection with the disposal of the above net assets, the Company's Board of Directors approved a quasi-reorganization (effective as of September 30, 1985) pursuant to which the Company's assets and liabilities were restated to estimated fair values (see Notes 2 and 3).

• • • •

At September 30, 1985, property, plant, and equipment was adjusted in connection with the quasi-reorganization (see Note 3).

• • • •

At September 30, 1985, property held for development was adjusted in connection with the quasi-reorganization (see Note 3).

• • • •

3. Quasi-Reorganization

In connection with the disposal of the net assets described in Note 2, the Company's Board of Directors approved a quasi-reorganization (effective as of September 30, 1985) pursuant to which the Company's assets and liabilities were restated to estimated fair values. The most significant adjustments to the continuing assets were an increase in property, plant and equipment of approximately $8,000,000 and a decrease in property held for development of approximately $1,800,000. In connection with the quasi-reorganization, the accumulated deficit of $50,344,000 was transferred to capital in excess of par value.

• • • •

GAMING AND TECHNOLOGY, INC. AND SUBSIDIARIES

Consolidated Balance Sheets
September 30, 1983 and 1982

	1983	1982
		Restated, Note 10
Shareholders' equity		
• • • •		
Common stock, $.10 par value; authorized 15,000,000 shares	957	937
Paid-in capital	467	368
Deficit since September 30, 1982	(1,172)	
	251	1,305
Less: Notes receivable from the sale of stock	123	116
	128	1,189

Consolidated Statements of Shareholders' Equity
Years Ended September 30, 1983, 1982, and 1981

	Common Stock	Paid-In Capital (Restated Note 10)	Deficit As Previously Reported	Adjust-ments (Note 10)	As Restated
Balances, October 1, 1980	$1,069	$19,806	($12,856)	($ 78)	($12,935)
Shares issued for services	7	171			
Cancellation of notes (a) and related shares	(2)	(65)			
Net loss			(1,418)	(9)	(1,427)
Balances, September 30, 1981	1,075	19,912	(14,275)	(88)	(14,363)
Shares issued for services	10	19			
Cancellation of notes (a) and related shares (Note 7b)	(149)	(2,173)			
Net loss			(1,628)	(13)	(1,642)
Adjustment to assets and liabilities and elimination of deficit through quasi-reorganization (Note 2)		(17,287)			
Balances September 30, 1982, as previously reported	937	470	($15,903)	($101)	(101)
Prior period adjustment (Note 10)		(101)			101
Balances September 30, 1982, as restated	937	368			
Shares issued for services	19	98			
Net loss					(1,172)
Balances, September 30, 1983	957	467			(1,172)
Shares issued for cash	480	720			
Pro forma balances September 30, 1983	$1,427	$ 1,187	$ 0	$ 0	($ 1,172)

Notes to Consolidated Financial Statements
Years Ended September 20, 1983, 1982, and 1981

1. Description of Activities and Summary of Significant Accounting Policies

• • • •

Property and equipment are generally stated at cost. Depreciation is provided by the straight-line method over the estimated useful lives of the assets, which in the case of leasehold improvements, is limited to the term of the lease. However, as of September 30, 1982, the date of the quasi-reorganization (Note 2), all accumulated depreciation was netted against the original cost, and further writedowns were taken, wherever applicable, to estimated realizable or salvage values for unproductive assets. No assets were written up in connection with the revaluation.

2. Quasi-Reorganization

On December 23, 1982, the Boards of Directors of the Company and all of its subsidiaries approved a corporate readjustment of their accounts, effected in the form of a quasi-reorganization, which resulted in a revaluation of all their assets and liabilities to estimated fair values and the elimination of the accumulated consolidated deficit, effective September 30, 1982. The Company obtained an opinion of counsel that Board of Directors' approval was sufficient to permit this action.

The net amount of such revaluation adjustments, together with the accumulated deficit as of the date thereof, was transferred to paid-in capital in accordance with the accounting principles applicable to quasi-reorganizations. The adjustments consisted principally of writedowns of certain gaming machines, which are not producing revenues due to technological obsolescence, the write-off of deferred costs not considered to have future value, including pre-opening costs of the Colorado Belle Casino and certain patents and other intangibles, the adjustment of debts to reflect current interest rates and the elimination of previously accrued settlement costs resulting from the voided settlement agreement with a former officer/director (Note 8a). Such assets were purchased by or committed to by prior management, as were two significant debt obligations which bear unfavorable interest rates, even as compared to prevalent rates at the time of the commitment.

The effect of the quasi-reorganization will be to reduce the burden of depreciation and interest charges on future operations resulting from these commitments made by prior management and, accordingly, will affect the comparability of future operating statements with those for years ending through September 30, 1982. Any gains or losses resulting from the ultimate disposition of revalued assets or liabilities, and any income tax benefits resulting from utilization in subsequent years of net operating loss and other carryforwards existing at September 30, 1982, will be excluded from results of operations and credited (or charged) to paid-in capital. Such tax carryforwards are detailed in Note 10.

• • • •

GREAT SOUTHWEST INDUSTRIES CORP. AND SUBSIDIARIES

Consolidated Balance Sheets
December 31, 1984 and 1983

	1984	1983
Stockholders' equity (deficit) (Notes 3, 11 and 12):		
Preferred stock, $20 par value. Authorized 2,500,000 shares; issued and outstanding 429,282 shares at December 31, 1984 and 59,482 shares at December 31, 1983, less discounts of $6,997,000 and $727,000, respectively	1,589	463
Common stock, $.10 par value. Authorized 15,000,000 shares; issued and outstanding 4,379,597 shares and 2,378,597 shares at December 31, 1984 and 1983, respectively	438	238
Paid-in capital	2,699	5,074
Accumulated deficit		(11,676)
Accumulated deficit from July 1, 1984, date of quasi-reorganization (Note 3)	(1,498)	
Total stockholders' equity (deficit)	3,228	(5,901)

Consolidated Statements of Stockholders' Equity (Deficit)
Years Ended December 31, 1984, 1983, and 1982

	Preferred Stock	Discount on Preferred Stock	Common Stock	Paid-In Capital	Retained Earnings (Deficit)
Balance as of December 31, 1981	$3,004	$(1,834)	$221	$ 4,408	$ 2,364
• • • •					
Balance as of December 31, 1983	1,190	(727)	238	5,074	(11,676)
Issuance of 50,000 shares of Series "H" preferred stock $20 par, in conjunction with sale of Tex-A-Mation	1,000				
Net loss for the six months ended June 30, 1984					(3,031)
Transactions related to debt restructures and quasi-reorganization:					
Issuance of 2,001,000 shares of common stock to Collins Well Service shareholders, principal lending bank and Selected Resources in conjunction with the debt restructure and dissolution of GSEC			200	50	
Issuance of 318,800 shares of Series "BB" preferred stock $20 par, to principal lending bank	6,376	(6,270)			
Issuance of 200,000 shares of Series "CC" preferred stock $20 par, to principal lending bank	4,000	(3,969)			
Issuance of 1,000 shares of Series "DD" preferred stock $20 par, to Selected Resources in conjunction with the purchase of the 10% minority interest in GSEC	20				
Debt restructure and revaluation of assets and liabilities in conjunction with quasi-reorganization	(4,000)	3,969		12,282	
Transfer of accumulated deficit to paid-in capital in conjunction with quasi-reorganization				(14,707)	14,707
Balance July 1, 1984 (effective date of quasi-reorganization)	8,586	(6,997)	438	2,699	
Net loss for the six months ended December 31, 1984					(1,498)
Balance as of December 31, 1984	$8,586	$(6,997)	$438	$ 2,699	$ (1,498)

Notes to Consolidated Financial Statements
December 31, 1984, 1983, and 1982

1. Summary of Significant Accounting Policies

a. Principles of Consolidation

• • • •

(3) Quasi-Reorganization and Debt Restructure

In conjunction with its comprehensive debt restructuring in July 1984, the Company, with the approval of its Board of Directors, revalued its assets and liabilities to estimated fair values and implemented a quasi-reorganization effective July 1, 1984. In conducting the revaluation, management utilized the services of outside appraisers and an investment banker/advisor. Adjustments are summarized as follows:

Indebtedness released including deferred and defaulted interest:	
Bank debt included in:	
Long-term debt	$ 4,954,000
Liabilities of discontinued operations	8,341,000
Due to sellers of acquired businesses	4,518,000
Net assets of discontinued operations transferred to bank	(5,477,000)
Estimated fair value of securities issued:	
Preferred stock	(126,000)
Common stock	(250,000)
Fair value adjustments:	
Reduction in cost basis of property, plant and equipment	(903,000)
Discount on restructured bank debt	1,600,000
Provision for disposition costs	(375,000)
Net increase in paid-in capital	$12,282,000
Deficit charged to paid-in capital	$14,707,000

• • • •

MATTEL, INC. AND SUBSIDIARIES

Consolidated Balance Sheets
December 26, 1987 and December 27, 1986

	1987	1986
Shareholders' Equity		
Preferred and preference stock		92
Common stock $1 par value, 150,000,000 shares authorized; outstanding 47,655,555 shares at December 26, 1987 and 38,254,461 shares at December 27, 1986	47,656	38,254
Additional paid-in capital	55,880	218,375
Common stock warrants—$6.25 Series	1,000	1,000
Accumulated deficit		(141,410)
Currency translation adjustments		11,849
Total shareholders' equity	104,536	128,160

Consolidated Statements of Shareholders' Equity

(in thousands)	Preferred and Preference Stock	Common Stock	Additional Paid-In Capital	Common Stock Warrants	Accumulated (Deficit)
Balance, December 29, 1984, as previously reported	$2,470	$30,051	$269,749	$3,902	$(166,409)
Cumulative effect of the change in accounting for income taxes					(16,912)
Balance, December 29, 1984, as restated	2,470	30,051	269,749	3,902	(183,321)
Net income					78,725
Preferred stock dividends —$1.25 per share					(2,972)
Conversion of Series A Preferred stock to common stock	(2,372)	4,890	(4,188)		
Preference stock dividends average of $22.71 per share			433		(14,727)
Exercise of stock options		298	2,256		
Exercise of common stock warrants		178	711	(178)	
Balance, December 28, 1985	98	35,417	268,961	3,724	(122,295)
Net (loss)					(8,251)
Preference stock dividends —average of $5.70 per share					(3,585)
Redemption of Preference stock	(6)		(62,927)		
Series C Preference stock dividends—$0.79 per share					(7,279)
Exercise of stock options		234	1,805		
Exercise of common stock warrants		2,603	10,536	(2,724)	
Balance, December 27, 1986	92	38,254	218,375	1,000	(141,410)
Net (loss)					(113,163)
Series C Preference stock dividends—$0.16 per share					(1,438)
Exercise of stock options		167	1,273		
Conversion of Series C Preference stock	(92)	9,235	(9,143)		
Quasi-Reorganization adjustments:					
Revaluation of assets and liabilities, net			68,685		
Transfer to additional paid-in capital			(223,310)		256,011
Balance, December 26, 1987	$ 0	$47,656	$ 55,880	$1,000	$ 0

Notes to Consolidated Financial Statements

Note 1. Summary of Significant Accounting Policies

• • • •

Property, Plant and Equipment

• • • •

Also included in property, plant and equipment is approximately $6 million of land revalued as part of the quasi-reorganization (Note 2).

• • • •

Also included in capitalized leases is approximately $81 million relating to real property leases revalued as part of the quasi-reorganization (Note 2). These amounts will be amortized over the terms of the leases.

Note 2. Restructuring and Quasi-Reorganization

During fiscal 1987, in response to changes in market and industry conditions, the Company reassessed its business strategies and decided to emphasize its staple products of "Barbie," "Hot Wheels" and preschool toys, reduce its dependence on new promotional toy lines, discontinue investment participation in children's television programming and restructure its manufacturing and distribution activities. The Company also completed refinancing transactions which resulted in the repayment of certain high-cost debt.

Included in fiscal 1987 results of operations are costs and expenses of approximately $75.2 million and an extraordinary charge of $20.7 million pertaining to this restructuring. A gain of $10 million was also recognized from the sale of a manufacturing facility closed in fiscal 1986. These amounts relate primarily to reductions in productive capacity, realignment of the distribution network, refinancing and retirement of certain long-term indebtedness, corporate reorganization and costs associated with discontinuing product lines not compatible with the Company's new, long-term focus.

In connection with its restructuring, the Company, with the approval of the Board of Directors, implemented a quasi-reorganization effective December 26, 1987 and revalued certain of its assets and liabilities to fair values as of that date. The determination of fair values was based primarily upon analyses conducted by outside consultants.

The quasi-reorganization, which did not require the approval of the Company's shareholders, resulted in an increase in property, plant and equipment of $83 million, a decrease in long-term indebtedness of $5 million and recognition of deferred tax liabilities of $19 million relating to these revaluations. The net effect of these adjustments aggregating approximately $69 million was credited to additional paid-in capital.

Additionally, the accumulated deficit of approximately $256 million and the cumulative translation adjustment of approximately $33 million were transferred to additional paid-in capital. This deficit was attributable primarily to operations which were discontinued in prior years and the restructuring.

• • • •

ORION PICTURES CORPORATION

Consolidated Balance Sheets
February 29, 1984 and February 28, 1983
(in thousands)

	1984	1983
Shareholders' equity (Notes 2, 3, 4, 5, 6 and 7):		
Preferred stock (liquidation preference $1,347 at February 29, 1984:		
Series A	58	58
Series B	97	296
Class C Convertible Preference Stock (liquidation preference $8,629 at February 29, 1984)	7,058	8,528
Common Stock	2,352	1,748
Paid-in surplus	66,622	16,817
Retained earnings since February 28, 1982	12,144	5,327
Total shareholders' equity	88,331	32,774

Consolidated Statements of Common Stock, Paid-In Surplus, and Retained Earnings (Deficit)
(in thousands)

	Common Stock	Paid-In Surplus	Retained Earnings (Deficit)
Balance, February 28, 1981	$1,460	$49,384	$(61,173)
Net loss			(16,721)
Issuance of common stock:			
Conversion of 6% debentures	1	53	
Conversion of 10,765 shares of Series A preferred stock	14	145	
Conversion of 500 shares of Series B preferred stock	1	5	
Conversion of 96,636 shares of Class C preference stock	15	854	
Exercise of stock options	3	224	
Retirement of treasury stock	(14)	(224)	
Treasury stock exchange	(16)	(198)	
New issuance (Note 2)	250	5,750	
Issuance of warrants (Note 2)		4,472	
Quasi-Reorganization as of February 28, 1982 (Note 3):			
Adjustments, net		31,273	
Transfer of deficit to paid-in surplus		(77,894)	77,894
Balance, February 28, 1982	1,714	13,844	$ 0

Notes to Consolidated Financial Statements

• • • •

3. Quasi-Reorganization

Subsequent to the Capital Infusion Transaction and as of February 28, 1982, the Company effected a quasi-reorganization whereby the Company's assets and liabilities were restated to reflect estimated fair values (resulting in a net increase in paid-in surplus of $31,273,000) and the existing accumulated deficit was transferred to paid-in surplus. The determination of the fair value was based primarily upon evaluations and studies by various investment bankers and management.

UNDER BANKRUPTCY PROCEEDING

CONTINENTAL STEEL CORPORATION

Balance Sheet

	December 31	
	1983	1982
	(in thousands)	
Shareholders' equity (Note 11)		
Common stock, par value $1 per share; authorized 35,000,000 and 25,000,000 shares; issued 17,419,363 and 10,569,363 shares, including excess over par	63,367	50,446
Less unamortized prepaid compensation (Note 10)	(10,822)	
Retained earnings (deficit) (deficit of $48,120 eliminated at March 31, 1982) (Note 2)	(25,447)	(15,509)
Total shareholders' equity	27,098	34,937

Statement of Changes in Retained Earnings (Deficit)

| | For the Years Ended December 31 | | |
	1983	1982	1981
	(in thousands except for per share amounts)		
NET LOSS	(9,938)	(25,358)	(17,080)
Retained earnings (deficit) at beginning of year	(15,509)	(38,271)	(21,191)
Retained deficit eliminated at March 31, 1982 (Note 2)		48,120	
Retained earnings (deficit) at end of year	$(25,447)	$(15,509)	$(38,271)

Statement of Changes in Other Capital Accounts
for the Years Ended December 31, 1983, 1982, and 1981
(in thousands)

| | Common Stock (Including Excess Over Par) | | Treasury Shares (At Cost) | |
	Shares	Amount	Shares	Amount
Balance, January 1, 1981	5,428,116	$52,644	160,356	$1,221
Settlement of litigation and cancellations		(17)	(4,000)	(21)
Balance, December 31, 1981	5,428,116	$52,627	156,356	1,200
Recording of Reorganization and Quasi-Reorganization (Note 2):				
Issuance of Common Stock upon emergence from Chapter 11 proceedings	5,297,603	13,215		
Retained deficit eliminated at March 31, 1982		(48,120)		
Revaluation of assets and liabilities		33,924		
Cancellation of Treasury Stock	(156,356)	(1,200)	(156,356)	(1,200)
Balance, December 31, 1982	10,569,363	$50,446		
Issuance of Common Stock for hourly profit sharing plan (Note 10)	6,000,000	$11,115		
Issuance of Common Stock for salaried stock plan (Note 10)	850,000	1,806		
Balance, December 31, 1983	17,419,363	$63,367	$ 0	$ 0

Notes to Financial Statements

1. Significant Accounting Policies

A. Reorganization Proceedings. In 1982, the Company emerged from bankruptcy proceedings. In accordance with the terms of the reorganization plans, the Company's retained earnings deficit as of March 31, 1982, was eliminated by a transfer from additional paid-in capital. Additionally, the Company's creditors received distributions of cash, common stock and a $4,200,000 10% Convertible Subordinated Income Debenture. As a result of the stock distributed, former creditors acquired approximately 51% of the Company's outstanding stock and the right to convert the Convertible Subordinated Debenture into stock that would increase creditor ownership to approximately 63% of outstanding shares.

As more fully described in Note 2, in recognition of the change in ownership, the Company effected a quasi-reorganization and, accordingly, adjusted the carrying value of all assets and liabilities to their fair values as of March 31, 1982.

2. Emergence from Bankruptcy

On March 15, 1982, after obtaining the requisite vote of each class of creditors and other interests, the reorganization plans of the Company (then known as Penn-Dixie Industries and Penn-Dixie Steel

Corporation, a wholly-owned subsidiary of Penn-Dixie Industries) became final and the Company emerged from bankruptcy proceedings. In accordance with the terms of the reorganization plans, Penn-Dixie Steel was merged into Penn-Dixie Industries and the Company's name was changed to Continental Steel Corporation ("Continental" or the "Company").

The plans provided that the Company distribute $39,489,000 in cash, 5,297,603 shares of common stock and a $4,200,000 10% Convertible Subordinated Income Debenture to former creditors (including tax and other governmental authorities). Additionally, as a part of the reorganization plans, the Company agreed upon settlement of other liabilities, previously deferred pursuant to reorganization proceedings. The settlements provided for payment plans extending from four to six years from March 1982.

The number of common shares issued to each creditor was determined based on a formula contained in the reorganization plans. The shares were valued at $2.50 per share. Because the cancelled liabilities were greater than the value of the shares issued, an extraordinary gain of $2,452,000 was recorded.

The Company's retained deficit was eliminated as called for in the reorganization plans by the transfer from the capital in excess of par value account of an amount equal to said retained deficit as of March 31, 1982.

In recognition of the change in ownership of the Company as brought about by the emergence from Chapter 11 bankruptcy proceedings, management recommended and the Company's Board of Directors approved a quasi-reorganization to be effective as of March 31, 1982. Accordingly, all assets and liabilities of the Company were restated as of March 31, 1982, to their fair value resulting in an increase in shareholders' equity of $33,924,000.

• • • •

NUCORP ENERGY, INC.

Consolidated Balance Sheet
December 31, 1986

SHAREHOLDERS' EQUITY—Notes A, B and D

Common Stock, stated value $.05 per share; 3,000,000 shares authorized, 2,000,000 shares issued and outstanding	100
Capital in excess of stated value	6,280
Retained earnings (deficit) from August 1, 1986	(163)
TOTAL SHAREHOLDERS' EQUITY	6,217

Consolidated Statement of Changes in Stockholders' Equity
for the Period August 1, 1986 Through December 31, 1986

	Common Shares	Stock Amount	Capital in Excess of Stated Value	Retained Earnings (Deficit)
Issuance of Common Stock Notes A and B	2,000	$100	$6,280	
Net loss for the period				$(163)
	2,000	$100	$6,280	$(163)

Notes to Consolidated Financial Statements
December 31, 1986

Note A. Description of Business and Reorganization Proceedings

On July 27, 1982, the Company and certain of its subsidiaries filed voluntary petitions under Chapter 11 of the United States Bankruptcy Code (the "Bankruptcy Code"), in the United States Bankruptcy Court for the Southern District of California (the "Bankruptcy Court").

• • • •

The Company engaged in extensive negotiations with its creditors and other parties-in-interest toward achieving a plan of reorganization and a settlement of outstanding claims against the Company.

As a result of these negotiations, the Company filed with the Bankruptcy Court its Second Amended Joint Plan of Reorganization (which plan of reorganization, as amended, is hereinafter referred to as the "Plan") and the related Disclosure Statement. After appropriate Bankruptcy Court hearings to determine the adequacy of the information contained in the Disclosure Statement, the Plan was submitted to all creditors for solicitation of acceptances of the Plan. After the requisite acceptances were obtained and the Bankruptcy Court determined that the Plan satisfied applicable requirements of the Bankruptcy Code, the Bankruptcy Court confirmed the Plan on December 20, 1985, and the Plan was consummated on July 31, 1986.

The principal provisions of the Plan are as follows:

1. The operations of certain of the Company's oil and gas subsidiaries were reorganized and consolidated into one entity named Pin Oak Petroleum Inc. ("Pin Oak"). A 51% interest in the stock of Pin Oak was transferred to certain creditors in satisfaction of their claims and the Company received an option to purchase such interest.

2. Substantially all of the assets of the Company, except for its investments in the stock of its subsidiaries (including a 49% interest in Pin Oak) and the above mentioned option were transferred to an estate administrator pursuant to a trust for the benefit of holders of allowed claims.

3. The Company was discharged from any liability or debt that arose on or prior to July 31, 1986. In connection with the transfer of assets, the estate administrator assumed all of the obligations of the Company under the Plan and agreed to indemnify the Company against such obligations.

4. The Company issued to the respective trustees 2,000,000 shares of the Company's Common Stock and 1,000,000 warrants for the purchase of an additional 1,000,000 shares of Common Stock, all to be distributed to certain holders of pre-reorganization public debt.

Note B. Accounting for the Reorganization

On August 1, 1986, as a result of the reorganization of the Company, the remaining assets of the Company were written down to fair value. The fair value of the Company's investment in Pin Oak was recorded at the Company's ownership percentage of the net assets of Pin Oak at such date. As of such date the assets and liabilities of Pin Oak had been restated to reflect their fair values based primarily upon recent appraisals and petroleum engineering reports.

In accordance with accounting principles applicable to reorganizations, the Company's deficit in retained earnings at the date of reorganization was eliminated and the excess of the fair values of the net assets of the Company over the stated value of outstanding capital stock was assigned to capital in excess of stated value. Any tax benefits resulting from utilization in subsequent years of net operating loss and other tax-related carryforwards existing at the date of reorganization (see Note F) will be excluded from operations and credited to capital in excess of stated value in the year utilized.

APPENDIX A

USING NAARS TO EXPAND THE INFORMATION IN THIS PUBLICATION

The National Automated Accounting Research System (NAARS) is a full-text, on-line data base, which includes three types of files: (1) corporate annual reports, (2) governmental units, and (3) accounting literature.

The corporate annual report files contain the financial statements, audit report, management responsibility letter, and footnotes. If the annual report received at the AICPA was a form 10-K, we also include the supplementary schedules and the exhibit on earnings per share.

There always are five single-year files of annual reports on-line, which may be searched individually or in a combined group. Each single-year file contains approximately 4,200 reports. The combined group contains over 21,000 annual reports.

SEARCH FRAMES

The reports in each file may be searched by employing a key word or phrase in the search frame transmitted. However, a particular accounting concept may be difficult to find by using a key word or phrase. For example, the subject Accounting Changes is sometimes difficult to identify in an annual report. A particular report may refer to an accounting change simply by saying; "During the year we changed the method of accounting for...," which is a simple example to find. The search frame to transmit may be constructed as follows:

CHANG! W/5 METHOD OR ACCOUNTING

In this case, the computer is instructed to search the annual reports for examples where any form of the word **CHANGE** (the exclamation point is a wild card) is found to appear within five words of either **METHOD** or **ACCOUNTING**.

However, a report that discloses an accounting change in a manner that does not use the word **CHANGE** can be a difficult one to find. For example, the report might say "Since 1986 we account for..." or "prior to 1985, we accounted for...." Both methods of disclosure imply there has been a change in the method of accounting but neither employ any form of the word **CHANGE**.

AICPA staff members index the footnotes to make it possible to find examples such as this one. Every footnote entered into the data base is read by a CPA at the Institute. These professionals identify accounting concepts contained within a footnote. The accounting concepts contained within the footnote are indexed by applying acronym(s) at the beginning of each note. When the report is entered into the data base, the acronym becomes part of the footnote. The acronyms are called *descriptors*. (A list of all the descriptors used in NAARS is presented below.) The descriptor that identifies an accounting change is **ACCTG**.

The above example may be searched by using the following search frame:

ACCTG W/SEG SINCE OR PRIOR OR CHANG! OR ADOPT!
W/5 METHOD OR ACCOUNT!

Here the computer is instructed to find examples of footnote disclosure, where the footnote includes the descriptor **ACCTG** and within the text of the footnote, the words **PRIOR** or **SINCE** or any form of the words **CHANGE** or **ADOPT** is found to appear within five words of **METHOD** or any form of the word **ACCOUNT**.

The descriptors also may be employed with a key word or phrase to find examples of specific kinds of changes. For example, the following search frame would provide examples of a change in the method of accounting for pension costs in conformity with Financial Accounting Standards Board Statement No. 87:

ACCTG W/SEG PENS W/SEG
(STATEMENT OR STANDARD OR SFAS OR FASB W/3 87)

At first glance, these search frames may appear intimidating. However, formulating a search becomes easy with a little experience. To provide new users with a quick-start, the AICPA is offering self-study courses on how to formulate searches and how to use this data base.

The course titles are as follows and are available from the AICPA Order Department 1-800-334-6961 (in New York, 1-800-248-0445):

Learning LEXIS/NEXIS/NAARS

Tax Research Using LEXIS/NEXIS/NAARS

Researching Corporate Accounting and Audit Problems on NAARS

(If you have questions about subscribing to the NAARS data base through AICPA TOTAL (Total On-line Tax and Accounting Library Service) call Hal G. Clark at 1-212-575-6893. To subscribe to TOTAL, call the Order Department number listed above.) *201-938-3248*

SEARCH FRAME USED FOR THIS SURVEY

Leonard Lorensen 201-938-3249

The following search frame was used to find the examples included in this survey:

(QUASIREORG! OR QUASI REORG!) OR (ELIMINAT! OR TRANSFER! OR OFFSET! OR RECLAS! OR CHARGE! W/8 DEFICIT) AND CAPCHG (EQUITY OR STOCK OR EARNINGS OR DEFICIT) OR EQUIT (EQUITY OR STOCK) OR REORG *[Some firms did the procedure but didn't call it a QR]*

The frame was used to instruct the computer to list the names of all companies in the files whose financial statements disclosed a note containing either one of two spellings of the word *quasi-reorganization*, or any form of the word *eliminate* or *transfer* or *offset* or *reclassify* or *charge* within eight words of the word *deficit*. Most such notes disclosed quasi-reorganizations as defined in the AICPA Issues Paper.

The frame also was used to instruct the computer to print this information contained in the financial statements of the companies disclosing quasi-reorganizations that were selected for this survey:

1. The note disclosing information about the quasi-reorganization
2. The statement of changes in stockholders' equity
3. The stockholders' equity section of the balance sheet

Items 2. and 3. contain additional information about the accounting for the quasi-reorganization.

The preceding search frame can be used to find additional examples of quasi-reorganizations in the files.

LIST OF DESCRIPTORS USED IN NAARS

Below is a listing of footnote descriptors used within the NAARS data base and a brief explanation of the concept identified by each:

Descriptor	Concept
PRACT	Accounting policies or practices
ACCTG	Accounting changes; changes in estimate
ACQUIS	Business combinations and acquisitions
COMMT	Commitments and contingencies
COMPEN	Compensation
CONSPOL	Consolidation policies
CONTR	Long-term contracts or lessor disclosures
DEBTAC	Debt
DEFERC	Deferred charges or credits; or negative goodwill
DIF	Disagreement between registrant and auditor
DISCOP	Discontinued operations disclosed within a footnote and the discontinued operation is presented as a separate segment in the income statement
DISCOPNSG	Discontinued operations disclosed within a footnote, and the discontinued operation is not presented as a separate segment in the income statement
EPS	Earnings per share
FORCST	Forecasting
FOREFF	Foreign exchange—economic effect
FORX	Foreign exchange
FYCHG	fiscal year change
FYDIF	Year end difference between investor/investee

INSIDR	Related party transactions
INTANG	Intangible assets—positive goodwill
INTCONT	Internal control
INTRIM	Quarterly information
INVOL	Involuntary conversion
LOB	Line of business or segment disclosure
MDA	Management and discussion analysis
NSUMOP	Notes to the summary of operations
PENS	Pension or retirement plans
PRIPER	Prior period adjustments
PROP	Property, depreciation, or depletion
REC	Receivables
RECLAS	Reclassifications
REORG	Reorganization or recapitalization
REPL	Replacement costs or current value of inflation disclosure
RESDEV	Research and development
REVREC	Revenue recognition
RRA	Reserve recognition accounting
STOK	Stock, shares, retained earnings, or dividends
STOKOP	Stock options
SUBEV	Subsequent event
SUPINF	Supplementary information
TX	Taxes
XTRA	Extraordinary items

In addition to the above footnote descriptors, the following are used to index or identify accounting concepts within the audit reports:

ADVER	Adverse opinion
CHGAUD	Change of auditor
CHGOP	Change prior year opinion
CONST	Consistency exception
CONTG	Contingency qualification
DISCL	Disclaimed opinion

GAAP	Departure from generally accepted accounting principles
INFDIS	Informative disclosure
OTHEX	Other reports, i.e., appraiser
RELYAUD	Reliance on other auditor
SCOP	Scope limitation
SUMOP	Summary of Operations covered by audit report
UNQUAL	Unqualified opinion

APPENDIX B

AUTHORITATIVE LITERATURE

The NAARS library contains a full-text file of authoritative and semi-authoritative accounting and auditing literature, which includes the following:

APB Opinions, Statements and Interpretations; Accounting Research Bulletins; Terminology Bulletins; Statements on Auditing Standards; Auditing Interpretations; Accounting Standards Executive Committee Pronouncements; Issues Papers; Industry Audit and Accounting Guides; Statements on Standards for Accounting and Review Services, and Interpretations; Statement on Quality Control and Interpretation; Statement on Management Advisory Service; Statement on Standards for Accountants' Services on Prospective Financial Information; Statement on Standards for Attestation Engagements; International Accounting Standard Committee Pronouncements; International Federation of Accountants Committee Pronouncements (Auditing); FASB Statements, Concepts, Interpretations and Technical Bulletins; FASB Emerging Issues Task Force Issues Summaries and Minutes of Meetings; Cost Accounting Standards Board Pronouncements; S.E.C. Staff Accounting Bulletins, Accounting Series Releases, Financial Reporting Releases, and Accounting and Auditing Enforcement Releases; AICPA Ethics—Concepts, Rules of Conduct, Interpretations, and Ethics Rulings—Technical Information Service Inquiries and Replies; GASB Statements, Interpretations, Technical Bulletins and Concepts; Office of Management and Budget Circulars and Standards for Audit of Governmental Organizations & Functions; Governmental Auditing Standards; Presidents Council on Integrity and Efficiency: State Network Block Grants

Just as search frames can be used to obtain illustrations of specific kinds of accounting from the NAARS annual report file, as discussed in appendix A, so can they be used to obtain currently effective authoritative guidance on specific accounting or auditing problems from the NAARS literature file. The following search frame was used to obtain currently effective authoritative guidance on quasi-reorganizations, the subject of this survey:

QUASI-REORG! OR QUASIREORG!

Most of the references obtained in the search are described in the AICPA Issues Paper on quasi-reorganizations, which is summarized in chapter 1 and reproduced as appendix C of this survey. The following references, obtained in the search, are not referred to in the Issues Paper:

1. Technical Practice Aids (TPA), Technical Information Service Inquiries and Replies (TIS), Section 4220.02, "Combining Paid-In Capital With Operating Deficit in the Absence of Quasi-reorganization." It discusses the accounting for such a combination in specified circumstances.

2. TPA, TIS, Section 4220.03, "Write-off of Accumulated Deficit After Quasi-reorganization." It discusses such a write-off in specified circumstances.

APPENDIX C

ISSUES PAPER 88-1

QUASI-REORGANIZATIONS

September 22, 1988

Prepared by the Quasi-Reorganizations Task Force
Accounting Standards Division
American Institute of Certified Public Accountants

NOTICE TO READERS

This issues paper is a research document intended for use by the Financial Accounting Standards Board and the Governmental Accounting Standards Board. Not all the alternative accounting methods and criteria described in the paper necessarily comply with generally accepted accounting principles. Accordingly, this issues paper is not intended to provide guidance on the preferability of accounting principles.

Introduction

The Accounting Standards Executive Committee's Task Force on Quasi-reorganizations has developed this issues paper to restudy the accounting procedures called quasi-reorganization.

Need for Project

The term quasi-reorganization is currently used to denote two accounting procedures, both of which involve the concept of an accounting fresh start, but whose importance and pervasiveness in financial reporting can differ considerably. The simpler of the two procedures is limited to a reclassification of a deficit in reported retained earnings as a reduction of paid-in capital. In addition to such a reclassification, the other procedure includes restatement of the carrying amounts of assets and liabilities. Clarification is needed as to

o Whether one or the other or both of the procedures should be permitted or required,

o What criteria should be met for each of the procedures to be permitted or required, and

o Whether the two procedures should be alternatives.

Present authoritative literature on quasi-reorganizations predates several important evolutionary steps in present generally accepted accounting principles related to procedures involving restatements of assets and liabilities, for example,

o The clean surplus theory adopted by APB Opinion 9,

o The detailed rules specified in APB Opinion 16 for accounting for business combinations using the purchase method,

o Experimentation with supplementary disclosure of information on changing prices, and

o The use of pushdown accounting in certain circumstances involving a change in the ownership of a reporting entity.

Further, formally reorganized companies emerging from bankruptcy only infrequently restate their assets and liabilities, and, if they do, the restatement is often referred to as a quasi-reorganization. Thus a formal reorganization does not generally result in restatement, but the term quasi-reorganization, which suggests an accounting simulation of a formal reorganization, is used to refer to a restatement.

Moreover, the authoritative literature in this area is permissive rather than mandatory, whereas financial accounting standards are now generally mandatory. Further, there are financial accounting and reporting issues concerning quasi-reorganizations for which the authoritative accounting literature provides no guidance or for which the guidance provided is unclear or conflicting.

Income Taxes

There are a number of issues in quasi-reorganizations on accounting for income taxes, such as how operating loss carryforwards and investment tax credit carryforwards should be accounted for after a quasi-reorganization. Those issues are not dealt with in this issues paper. The FASB has issued Statement No. 96, "Accounting for Income Taxes," which significantly changes existing standards for accounting for income taxes. Paragraph 54 of that Statement deals with accounting for the tax benefits of carryforwards subsequent to a quasi-reorganization. (See "Authoritative Literature and SEC Releases" below.) Questions have arisen as to how to interpret paragraph 54, and the FASB staff may provide guidance in a Questions and Answers booklet. In issuing Statement No. 96, the Board did not readdress basic issues in quasi-reorganizations. Certain conclusions on certain issues in this paper would suggest that paragraph 54 should be reconsidered. It was considered that the usefulness of this issues paper would not be measurably improved by a discussion of possible changes in accounting for income taxes that might be suggested by the resolution of the various issues in the paper.

History of Quasi-Reorganizations

According to James Schindler's 1958 study, <u>Quasi-reorgani-zation</u>[1], the quasi-reorganization had its beginnings in the write-ups of the 1920s. At that time, managements determined that the depreciated cost bases of land, buildings, and equipment did not reflect their current values and adjusted assets upward to appraised amounts. Schindler stated that the practice followed this pattern:

> To the extent that an explanation, if any, was made with respect to a write-up, usually it was a brief statement indicating that an "appraisal" had been made. This explanation, it is apparent, has little if any direct meaning, especially when the appraisal, usually implying an independent appraisal, was prepared after reaching the decision to revalue the assets. The statement that there was a discrepancy between book value and "present value" likewise offered little assistance to indicate why the revaluation action was taken by the management at that particular time. (p. 12)

A 1928 survey by the American Institute of Accountants (later AICPA) indicated that 85% of those surveyed believed the results of write-ups should not be recorded in income for the period. Similarly, according to Schindler:

---

[1] James S. Schindler, <u>Quasi-reorganization</u>, Ann Arbor, Michigan, University of Michigan, School of Business Administration, 1958.

102

The view favored by most accountants throughout the 1920's was that the income statement and the earned surplus account were to reflect the cost basis even though appreciation had been recognized. That is, depreciation on cost should be charged to the profit and loss account and depreciation on the appreciation increase should be charged to the recorded appraisal surplus or reserve account. (p. 27)

From 1930 to 1934, many companies wrote down their assets. As Warren Nissley explained in the April 1933 _Journal of Accountancy_:

I think that the outstanding effect... of the happenings of 1932, on balance sheets and income accounts will be the burial of the remains of that period once described as the "new era." In most cases, the statements will show the interment in the full light of day because such burials are fashionable now and appear to cause little criticism. Most executives appear to think that those errors of judgment during the 'new era,' which were the cause of the major adjustments now necessary in the accounts of their companies, were errors universally made by all managements. And they realize that if these adjustments are not made now, they will have to be made in the future. So far as the adjustments apply entirely to the past, it appears proper to clean house now, but it is important to ascertain whether or not any of them are designed to relieve the future of any charges that should properly be borne by later periods. (pp. 283-84)

That led to the adoption of the AICPA's Rule No. 2 of 1934 as it appears in ARB No. 43, Chapter 7A. At about the same time, the newly formed Securities and Exchange Commission issued Accounting Series Releases (ASR) Nos. 1, 15, and 16, and in 1941, ASR No. 25. Those pronouncements and others are discussed in the next section.

Authoritative Literature and SEC Releases

Quasi-reorganizations are addressed in ARB No. 43, chapter 7A, which states:

1. A rule was adopted by the Institute in 1934 which read as follows:

> Capital surplus, however created, should not be used to relieve the income account of the current or future years of charges which would otherwise fall to be made thereagainst. This rule might be subject to the exception that where upon reorganization, a reorganized company would be relieved of charges which would require to be made against income if the existing corporation were continued, it might be regarded as permissible to accomplish the same result without reorganization provided the facts were as fully revealed to and the action as formally approved by the shareholders as in reorganizations.

2. Readjustments of the kind mentioned in the exception to the rule fall in the category of what are called quasi-reorganizations. This section does not deal with the general question of quasi-reorganizations, but only with cases in which the exception permitted under the rule of 1934 is availed of by a corporation. Hereinafter such cases are referred to as readjustments. The problems which arise fall into two groups: (a) what may be permitted in a readjustment and (b) what may be permitted thereafter.

Procedure in Readjustment

3. If a corporation elects to restate its assets, capital stock, and surplus through a readjustment and thus avail itself of permission to relieve its future income account or earned surplus account of charges which would otherwise be made thereagainst, it should make a clear report to its shareholders of the restatements proposed to be made, and obtain their formal consent. It should present a fair balance sheet as at the date of the readjustment, in

which the adjustment of carrying amounts is reasonably complete, in order that there may be no continuation of the circumstances which justify charges to capital surplus.

4. A write-down of assets below amounts which are likely to be realized thereafter, though it may result in conservatism in the balance sheet at the readjustment date, may also result in overstatement of earnings or of earned surplus when the assets are subsequently realized. Therefore, in general, assets should be carried forward as of the date of readjustment at fair and not unduly conservative amounts determined with due regard for the accounting to be employed by the company thereafter. If the fair value of any asset is not readily determinable a conservative estimate may be made, but in that case the amount should be described as an estimate and any material difference arising through realization or otherwise and not attributable to events occurring or circumstances arising after that date should not be carried to income or earned surplus.

5. Similarly, if potential losses or charges are known to have arisen prior to the date of readjustment but the amounts thereof are then indeterminate, provision may properly be made to cover the maximum probable losses or charges. If the amounts provided are subsequently found to have been excessive or insufficient, the difference should not be carried to earned surplus nor used to offset losses or gains originating after the readjustment, but should be carried to capital surplus.

6. When the amounts to be written off in a readjustment have been determined, they should be charged first against earned surplus to the full extent of such surplus; any balance may then be charged against capital surplus. A company which has subsidiaries should apply this rule in such a way that no consolidated earned surplus survives a readjustment in which any part of losses has been charged to capital surplus.

7. If the earned surplus of any subsidiaries cannot be applied against the losses before resort is had to capital surplus, the parent company's interest in

such earned surplus should be regarded as capitalized by the readjustment just as surplus at the date of acquisition is capitalized, so far as the parent is concerned.

8. The effective date of the readjustment, from which the income of the company is thereafter determined, should be as near as practicable to the date on which formal consent of the stockholders is given, and should ordinarily not be prior to the close of the last completed fiscal year.

Procedure after Readjustment

9. When the readjustment has been completed, the company's accounting should be substantially similar to that appropriate for a new company.

10. After such a readjustment earned surplus previously accumulated cannot properly be carried forward under that title. A new earned surplus account should be established, dated to show that it runs from the effective date of the readjustment, and this dating should be disclosed in financial statements until such time as the effective date is no longer deemed to possess any special significance.

11. Capital surplus originating in such a readjustment is restricted in the same manner as that of a new corporation; charges against it should be only those which may properly be made against the initial surplus of a new corporation.

12. It is recognized that charges against capital surplus may take place in other types of readjustments to which the foregoing provisions would have no application. Such cases would include readjustments for the purpose of correcting erroneous credits made to capital surplus in the past. In this statement the committee has dealt only with that type of readjustment in which either the current income or earned surplus account or the income account of future years is relieved of charges which would otherwise be made thereagainst.

ARB No. 43, Chapter 9(b), as amended by APB Opinion No. 6,

states that:

> property, plant and equipment should not be
> written up by an entity to reflect appraisal,
> market or current values which are above cost
> to the entity. This statement is not intended
> to change accounting practices followed in
> connection with quasi-reorganizations or
> reorganizations...Whenever appreciation has
> been recorded on the books, income should be
> charged with depreciation computed on the
> written up amounts.

ARB No. 46 amended paragraph 10 of ARB No. 43, Chapter 7(a) to indicate that dating of retained earnings "would rarely, if ever, be of significance after a period of ten years." SEC Regulation S-X Rule 5-02.31 requires dating of retained earnings for 10 years and disclosure of the amount of deficit eliminated for 3 years.

APB Opinion 9, paragraph 28, states that adjustments made pursuant to a quasi-reorganization should be excluded from the determination of net income or the results of operations under all circumstances. The Opinion deals only with entries giving effect to the quasi-reorganization and does not deal with effects on postquasi-reorganization reporting of adjustments made pursuant to the quasi-reorganization, for example, depreciation on assets whose carrying amounts have been restated.

Accounting for the tax benefits of net operating loss carryforwards emerging before quasi-reorganizations is addressed in APB Opinion 11, paragraph 50, which states that the tax effects of loss carryforwards arising prior to a quasi-reorganization (including for this purpose the application of a deficit in retained earnings to contributed capital) should, if not previously recognized, be recorded as assets at the date of the quasi-reorganization only if realization is assured beyond any reasonable doubt. If not previously recognized and the benefits are actually realized at a later date, the tax effects should be added to contributed capital because the benefits are attributable to the loss periods prior to the quasi-reorganization.

AICPA Accounting Interpretation of APB Opinion 11, No. 8 states that permanent tax differences frequently result from "writedowns of assets in a reorganization."

FASB Statement No. 96 supersedes APB Opinion 11 effective for fiscal years beginning after December 15, 1988. Paragraph 54 of that Statement provides:

The tax benefit of an operating loss or tax credit carryforward for financial reporting as of the date of the quasi reorganization as defined and contemplated (involving write-offs directly to contributed capital) in ARB No. 43, Chapter 7, "Capital Accounts," is reported as a direct addition to contributed capital if the tax benefits are recognized in subsequent years. Some quasi reorganizations involve only the elimination of a deficit in retained earnings by a concurrent reduction in contributed capital. For that type of reorganization, subsequent recognition of the tax benefit of a prior operating loss or tax credit carryforward for financial reporting is reported as required by paragraph 52 and then reclassified from retained earnings to contributed capital. Regardless of whether the reorganization is labeled as a quasi reorganization, if prior losses were charged directly to contributed capital, the subsequent recognition of a tax benefit for a prior operating loss or tax credit carryforward for financial reporting is reported as a direct addition to contributed capital.

(Under paragraph 52, the manner of reporting the tax benefit of a loss carryforward is determined by the source of income in the current year, that is, the year in which the carryforward is utilized.)

FASB Statement No. 15, "Accounting by Debtors and Creditors for Troubled Debt Restructurings" indicates that it does not apply to a quasi-reorganization with which a troubled debt restructuring coincides if "the debtor restates its liabilities generally."

The Securities and Exchange Commission has issued various Accounting Series Releases on quasi-reorganizations. The most recent is ASR No. 25 (FRR 210), issued May 29, 1941, which states:

> It has been the Commission's view for some time that a quasi-reorganization may not be considered to have been effected unless at least all of the following conditions exist:
>
> (1) Earned surplus, as of the date selected, is exhausted;
>
> (2) Upon consummation of the quasi-reorganization, no deficit exists in any surplus account;
>
> (3) The entire procedure is made known to all persons entitled to vote on matters of general corporate policy and the appropriate consents to the particular transactions are obtained in advance in accordance

with the applicable law and charter provisions;

(4) The procedure accomplishes, with respect to the accounts, substantially what might be accomplished in a reorganization by legal proceedings--namely, the restatement of assets in terms of present conditions as well as appropriate modifications of capital and capital surplus, in order to obviate so far as possible the necessity of future reorganizations of like nature.

It is implicit in such a procedure that reductions in the carrying value of assets at the effective date may not be made beyond a point which gives appropriate recognition to conditions which appear to have resulted in relatively permanent reductions in asset values; as for example, complete or partial obsolescence, lessened utility value, reduction in investment value due to changed economic conditions, or, in the case of current assets, declines in indicated realization value. It is also implicit in a procedure of this kind that it is not to be employed recurrently but only under circumstances which would justify an actual reorganization or formation of a new corporation, particularly if the sole or principal purpose of the quasi-reorganization is the elimination of a deficit in earned surplus resulting from operating losses.

In the case of the quasi-reorganization of a parent company, it is an implicit result of such procedure that the effective date should be recognized as having the significance of a date of acquisition of control of subsidiaries. Likewise, in consolidated statements, earned surplus of subsidiaries at the effective date should be excluded from earned surplus on the consolidated balance sheet.

Previous ASRs related to quasi-reorganizations and asset revaluation included these:

o ASR No. 1 (4/1/37), "Treatment of Losses Resulting

from Revaluation of Assets." The Chief Accountant
states,

> To my mind, the revaluation of the assets
> involved was simply a recognition by the
> company, as of the date of the write-down,
> of an accumulation of depreciation in val-
> ues incidental to the risks involved in the
> ordinary operation of its business. This
> depreciation did not occur as of a given
> date; it took place gradually over a period
> of years coincident with the evolution of
> the industry. Thus it was an element of
> production costs applicable to an indefin-
> ite period prior to the write-down and as
> such would have been charged against income
> had it been discerned and provided for
> currently.

> It is my conviction that capital surplus
> should under no circumstances be used to
> write off losses which, if currently recog-
> nized, would have been chargeable against
> income. In case a deficit is thereby
> created, I see no objection to writing off
> such a deficit against capital surplus,
> provided appropriate stockholder approval
> has been obtained. In this event, subse-
> quent statements of earned surplus should
> designate the point of time from which the
> new surplus dates. (Rescinded.)

o ASR No. 7 (5/16/38) - Cites common deficiencies in
  financial statements filed with the SEC including
  (1) use of capital to absorb writedowns in plant
  and equipment that should have been charged to
  earned surplus and (2) failure to date the earned
  surplus account after a deficit has been eliminated
  (with stockholders' approval) by a charge to capital surplus. (Rescinded.)

o ASR No. 8 (5/20/38), "Creation by Promotional Companies of Surplus by Appraisal." This ASR required
  a company to reverse a writeup of assets to appraised value. (Superseded by ASR 215-enforce-
  ment.)

o   ASR No. 15 (3/16/40), "Description of Surplus Ac-
    cruing Subsequent to Effective Date of Quasi-Reor-
    ganization," requires full disclosure of the ef-
    fects of quasi-reorganization for a minimum of
    three years. ASR No. 16 (3/16/40) would require
    specific disclosures in cases in which stockholder
    approval is not required. (Rescinded.)

o   ASR No. 50 (1/20/45), "The Propriety of Writing
    Down Goodwill by Means of Charges to Capital Sur-
    plus." Similarly to ASR No. 1, the ASR indicates
    writeoffs of goodwill to capital surplus are impro-
    per. (Rescinded.)

On August 25, 1988, the SEC staff issued Staff Accounting

Bulletin (SAB) 78 on quasi-reorganizations. The SAB states

> FACTS: As a consequence of significant operating
> losses and/or recent write-downs of property,
> plant and equipment, a company's financial state-
> ments reflect an accumulated deficit. The company
> desires to eliminate the deficit by reclassifying
> amounts from paid-in-capital. In addition, the
> company anticipates adopting a discretionary
> change in accounting principles[1] that will be
> recorded as a cumulative-effect type of accounting
> change. The recording of the cumulative effect
> will have the result of increasing the company's
> retained earnings.
>
> Question 1: May the company reclassify its capi-
> tal accounts to eliminate the accumulated deficit
> without satisfying all of the conditions enumera-

---

[1] Discretionary accounting changes require the
filing of a preferability letter by the registrant's independent accountant pursuant to Item
601 of Regulation S-K and Rule 10-01(b)(6) of
Regulation S-X, 17 CFR sections 229.601 and
210.10-01(b)(6), respectively.

ted in Section 210^2 of the Codification of Financial Reporting Policies for a quasi-reorganization?

Interpretive Response: No. The staff believes a deficit reclassification of any nature is considered to be a quasi-reorganization. As such, a company may not reclassify or eliminate a deficit in retained earnings unless all requisite conditions set forth in Section 210^3 for a quasi-reorganization are satisfied.^{4}

---

[2] Accounting Series Release No. 25 (May 29, 1941).

[3] Section 210 indicates the following conditions under which a quasi-reorganization can be effected without the creation of a new corporate entity and without the intervention of formal court proceedings:

(1) Earned surplus, as of the date selected, is exhausted;

(2) Upon consummation of the quasi-reorganization, no deficit exists in any surplus account;

(3) The entire procedure is made known to all persons entitled to vote on matters of general corporate policy and the appropriate consents to the particular transactions are obtained in advance in accordance with the applicable laws and charter provisions;

(4) The procedure accomplishes, with respect to the accounts, substantially what might be accomplished in a reorganization by legal proceedings--namely, the restatement of assets in terms of present conditions as well as appropriate modifications of capital and capital surplus, in order to obviate so far as possible the necessity of future reorganizations of like nature.

[4] In addition, Accounting Research Bulletin (ARB) No. 43, Chapter 7A, outlines procedures that must be followed in connection with and after a quasi-reorganization.

Question 2: Must the company implement the discretionary change in accounting principle simultaneously with the quasi-reorganization or may it adopt the change after the quasi-reorganization has been effected?

Interpretive Response: The staff has taken the position that the company should adopt the anticipated accounting change prior to or as an integral part of the quasi-reorganization. Any such accounting change should be effected by following generally accepted accounting principles with respect to the change.[5]

Chapter 7A of Accounting Research Bulletin (ARB) No. 43 indicates that, following a quasi-reorganization, a "company's accounting should be substantially similar to that appropriate for a new company." The staff believes that implicit in this "fresh-start" concept is the need for the company's accounting principles in place at the time of the quasi-reorganization to be those planned to be used following the reorganization to avoid a misstatement of earnings and retained earnings after the reorganization.[6] Chapter 7A of ARB No. 43 states, in part, "...in general, assets should be carried forward as of the date of the readjust-

---

[5] Accounting Principles Board Opinion No. 20 provides accounting principles to be followed when adopting accounting changes. In addition, many newly-issued accounting pronouncements provide specific guidance to be followed when adopting the accounting specified in such pronouncements.

[6] Certain newly-issued accounting standards do not require adoption until some future date. The staff believes, however, that if the registrant intends or is required to adopt those standards within 12 months following the quasi-reorganization, the registrant should adopt those standards prior to or as an integral part of the quasi-reorganization. Further, registrants should consider early adoption of standards with effective dates more than 12 months subsequent to a quasi-reorganization.

ment at fair and not unduly conservative amounts, <u>determined with due regard for the accounting to be employed by the Company thereafter</u> (emphasis added).

In addition, the staff believes that adopting a discretionary change in accounting principle that will be reflected in the financial statements within 12 months following the consummation of a quasi-reorganization leads to a presumption that the accounting change was contemplated at the time of the quasi-reorganization.[7]

Question 3: In connection with a quasi-reorganization, may there be a write-up of net assets?

Interpretive Response: No. The staff believes that increases in the recorded values of specific assets (or reductions in liabilities) to fair value are appropriate providing such adjustments are factually supportable, however, the amount of such increases are limited to offsetting adjustments to reflect decreases in other assets (or increases in liabilities) to reflect their new fair value. In other words, a quasi-reorganization should not result in a write-up of net assets of the registrant.

---

[7] Certain accounting changes require restatement of prior financial statements. The staff believes that if a quasi-reorganization has been recorded in a restated period, the effects of the accounting change on quasi-reorganization adjustments should also be restated to properly reflect the quasi-reorganization in the restated financial statements.

Generally, SAB 78 precludes a registrant from undertaking a quasi-reorganization that involves only a reclassification of the deficit in retained earnings to paid-in capital. The SAB re-affirms the condition of ASR No. 25 (Section 210 of the Codification of Financial Reporting Policies) that any quasi-reorganization should accomplish "the restatement of assets in terms of present conditions..." Thus, either the carrying amounts of all assets and liabilities must approximate their fair values at the date of the quasi-reorganization, or the quasi-reorganization must entail a revaluation of all assets and liabilities. According to the SEC staff, the SAB applies equally to companies emerging from formal reorganization (that is, bankruptcy) and other registrants.

The SAB specifically precludes a write-up of net assets. However, the SEC staff states that, in some cases, asset write-downs or similar losses recognized in income may be viewed as part of a quasi-reorganization if the timing and nature, relative to other revaluations reflected directly in equity, are such that they can be considered a single event. Thus, in some cases, it may be appropriate to consider such charges to income as one component and a net credit to equity for revaluation of other assets or liabilities as the other, provided that there is a resulting overall decrease in net assets. The staff of the SEC should be consulted in those instances.

Other Literature

In <u>A Concise Textbook on Legal Capital</u>, Bayless Manning discusses provisions of the Model Business Corporation Act related to quasi-reorganizations:

> The (Model Business Corporation Act) explicitly makes place for the so-called "quasi-reorganization." This strange term requires a little explanation. If the only permissible statutory basis for dividend payments is earned surplus, the management has a considerable incentive to avoid making other kinds of charges against "earned surplus" and, where some surplus charge must be made, to try to arrange for the charge to be made against some sub-category of "capital surplus" as defined in the statute. It would be nice, for example, if an uninsured fire loss could be charged against a paid-in surplus account, leaving the earned surplus account intact. That particular instance is denied by generally accepted accounting principles and met by the Model Act, for the definition of earned surplus makes it clear that the management will not be free to protect and immunize its earned surplus account in this fashion. But after having taken this step, Section 64 of the Act provides:
>
> 1. A corporation may, by resolution of its board of directors, apply any part or all of its capital surplus to the reduction or elimination of any deficit arising from losses, however incurred, but only after first eliminating earned surplus, if any, of the corporation by applying such losses against earned surplus and only to the extent that such losses exceed the earned surplus, if any.

Each such application of capital surplus shall, to the extent thereof, effect a reduction of capital surplus.

What this means is that a corporation that has distributed assets to shareholders to the full extent of its earned surplus and later develops a negative earned surplus, may then apply a portion of its capital surplus to the deficit to bring the deficit up to zero and thereafter pay out additional assets to its shareholders as soon as there are any earnings. As has been described earlier, capital surplus is not difficult to generate; a simple reduction of par or other reduction of stated capital will do it. The net result of these provisions of the Model Act, therefore, is that in addition to permitting direct distribution of capital surplus a corporation may, through use of capital surplus and an offset to deficit, pay all current earnings to its shareholders despite a deficit in the earned surplus account prior to the offset. Thus, by going through the right moves, capital surplus, or even stated capital can be set off against a corporate deficit. That is a so called "quasi-reorganization." The operational consequence is precisely antithetical to the creditor protection purposes of the stated capital scheme in general - and to the earned surplus standard in particular.[2]

Section 64 was renumbered and then deleted from the Model Act in 1979 in connection with basic revisions to the financial provisions of the Model Act. Those revisions included "(a) the elimination of the outmoded concepts of stated capital and par value, (b) the definition of 'distribution' as a broad term governing dividends, share repurchases and similar actions that should be governed by the same standard, [and] (c) the reformula-

---

[2] Bayless Manning, A Concise Textbook on Legal Capital (Mineola, New York: Foundation Press 1977), pp. 74-75.

tion of the statutory standards governing the making of distributions..."[3]

Prentice Hall's <u>Corporation Statutes</u> discusses the legality of charging dividends to revaluation surplus:

> Whether an increase in surplus arising from an increase in the value of the assets owned by the corporation is available for dividends, is highly controversial.
>
> Surplus is the excess of the aggregate value of all assets of a corporation over the sum of all its liabilities, including its capital stock. So in order to arrive at the amount of surplus from which dividends may be paid you must determine the value of the assets.
>
> Under conventional accounting practice, fixed assets are valued on the corporation's books at acquisition cost less depreciation; current assets at lower of cost or market value. But suppose the value of the assets has appreciated, although this appreciation hasn't been realized through a sale of the asset. Can the directors enter the appreciated value on the corporate books and thus create "revaluation surplus" from which dividends may be paid? The answer depends on (1) state law, (2) the kind of assets revalued, whether fixed or current, (3) the kind of dividends paid, whether cash or stock dividends, and whether on preferred or common.

---

[3] Committee on Corporate Laws, "Changes in the Model Business Corporation Act - Amendments to Financial Provisions," <u>The Business Lawyer</u>, 34, No. 4 (July 1979), 1867.

The first step toward an answer is to check the state statutes. Statutes in some states expressly prohibit the payment of cash or property dividends from unrealized appreciation in any kind of assets - others only from unrealized appreciation in fixed assets. Statutes in other states expressly or impliedly permit the payment of dividends from unrealized appreciation, but many require that stockholders be notified of the source of the dividend.

Court decisions are confusing. Many concern impairing capital by overcapitalization or fictitious writeup of assets, not actual appreciation in a general rise in prices. But generally courts have accepted the common law rule that unrealized appreciation in the value of fixed assets is not available for dividends.

An increase in the market price of the corporations' inventories would not be a proper source of dividends.(paragraph 2531 pp. 2517-2518)

Schindler discussed the relationship between state laws and accounting procedures for quasi-reorganizations:

The provisions of the state incorporation acts related to conditions precedent as well as to procedures to carry out such a reorganization have been accepted as minimum requirements to effect a quasi-reorganization. In the development of a formal quasi-reorganization procedure, the accounting profession attempted to prescribe conditions precedent to general applicability for effecting such a reorganization. When the legal conditions did not accomplish the accounting requirements, additional procedures were to be followed to meet recognized standards of accounting, or a quasi-reorganization was not deemed to have been effected.(pp. 50-51)

Issues and Arguments

Organization of Issues and Arguments Section and Terminology

The issues and arguments section of this paper is divided into two parts. Part I deals with quasi-reorganizations that result solely in eliminating deficits in reported retained earnings without restating assets or liabilities. Such quasi-reorganizations are referred to in the rest of this paper as <u>deficit reclassifications</u>. Part II deals with quasi-reorganizations that result both in eliminating a deficit and in restatements of assets or liabilities. Such quasi-reorganizations are referred to in the rest of this paper as <u>accounting reorganizations</u>.

Part I - Deficit Reclassification

ISSUE 1: Should a deficit reclassification ever be permitted?

Some believe a deficit reclassification should, under certain conditions, be permitted. They offer these reasons:

o Deficit reclassifications enable reporting entities that have the resources and the desire to pay dividends but are not permitted to do so under state law because of reported deficits in retained earnings to eliminate their reported deficits and to be permitted to pay dividends under state law. Many in the financial community believe the legal prohibition on paying dividends that could otherwise be paid causes unnecessary hardship for many reporting entities and their stockholders.

o Though many states allow payment of dividends to be charged to paid in capital, dividends charged to paid in capital may be perceived differently by the financial community from dividends charged to retained earnings, an unnecessary and unsatisfactory condition.

o Because subdividing equity according to its sources appears to be based on legal concepts and not accounting concepts, there is no reason to prohibit a change in that subdivision if the law permits it. FASB Concepts Statement No. 6, paragraph 49 defines equity as "the residual interest in the assets of an entity that remains after deducting its liabilities." Footnote 29 to that Statement states:

> This Statement defines equity of a business enterprise only as a whole, although the discussion notes that different owners of an enterprise may have different kinds of ownership rights and that equity has various sources. In financial statements of business enterprises, various distinctions within equity, such as those between...contributed capital and earned capital, or between stated or legal capital and other equity, are primarily matters of display...

Further, the reported amount of retained earnings or deficit provides incomplete and usually inconclusive information about legal restrictions on the payment of dividends. For example, in some states dividends may be charged against capital surplus; and typically, if treasury stock is not accounted for as retired, its cost reduces retained earnings available for dividends.

o   Apart from providing some inconclusive information about legal restrictions on payments of dividends, statistics about the sources of a reporting entity's equity provide little useful information. For many reporting entities those statistics have already been affected by capitalizations of earnings in connection with stock distributions, business combinations accounted for by the pooling of interests method, and the like. Further, though a deficit in reported retained earnings could result from cumulative losses from operations, a deficit is also a function of the reporting entity's dividend policy and the extent of, and the accounting for, its treasury stock transactions. The fact that there is a deficit, or its amount, may provide little useful information by itself.

o   If an entity could pay dividends by changing its state of incorporation, a deficit reclassification would permit such payment without incurring the cost of such a change.

o A deficit reclassification provides a means of formally recognizing contraction in the size of a reporting entity in terms of its stated capital.

o Permitting deficit reclassifications would allow managements to have fresh starts in reporting the discharge of their responsibilities to shareholders, which some believe is reflected in the amount of retained earnings or deficit.

Others believe a deficit reclassification should never be permitted. They offer these reasons:

o Reported retained earnings or deficit is a useful statistic reflecting historical transactions and its integrity should be protected.

o If reporting entities are permitted to reclassify deficits and start fresh in accumulating retained earnings, they may be encouraged to record discretionary expenses or losses before a deficit reclassification.

o Financial reporting should not attempt to change economic circumstances such as the ability to pay dividends; it should only describe changes that have occurred.

o It would be impossible to define with sufficient

clarity which circumstances should justify a deficit reclassification and thus the procedure would be largely discretionary.

o If a reclassification of a deficit is to be justified on the basis of a fresh start, it should not be confined solely to reclassification of equity accounts. Rather, it should occur only in an accounting reorganization, because only a complete restatement of the balance sheet is consistent with the fresh start objective.

o It is contended that presentations in balance sheets of separate amounts for paid in capital and retained earnings can be misleading:

> Because dividends are deducted from earnings and only the difference is presented, financial statements users can't tell from the balance sheet the amount of equity obtained from successful operations. They also can't tell from such a presentation when equity was obtained from its various sources. The amounts presented as components of equity can be misleading for both of those reasons.[4]

Because quasi-reorganizations further obscure the history the equity sections of balance sheets pur-

---

[4] Paul Rosenfield versus Steven Rubin, "Minority Interest: Opposing Views," <u>Journal of Accountancy</u>, March 1986, page 80.

port to present concerning the profitability of the reporting entities that record them, they make those sections even more misleading.

Conditions Under Which a Reporting Entity Should Be Permitted to Record a Deficit Reclassification

The following section discusses some of the possible criteria for permitting deficit reclassifications, assuming deficit reclassifications should be permitted.

ISSUE 2. **If a deficit reclassification should be permitted, should a reporting entity demonstrate a reasonable prospect of future profitability to qualify for a deficit reclassification?**

Some believe a deficit reclassification should not be permitted unless a reporting entity can demonstrate a reasonable prospect of future profitability, so that recurrence of a deficit is unlikely; otherwise it is pointless to provide a fresh accounting start.

Others believe that a reasonable prospect of future profitability should not have to be demonstrated. They believe that an accounting procedure should be beneficial to the users of the financial reports for it to be justified. If a deficit reclassification passes that test by leading to balance sheets that are more informative to the users, for example, by measuring retained earnings (deficit) from the date a fresh start is deemed to have occurred, that advantage should not be denied them merely because present indicators suggest that the reporting entity may not be profitable in the future. Further, they point out that satisfying such a condition would entail the reporting entity's auditors being able to conclude that a reasonable prospect of future profitability has been demonstrated.

ISSUE 3: **If a deficit in retained earnings should be required in order for a reporting entity to qualify for a deficit reclassification, what consideration, if any, should be given to separate accounts reported in equity that result from cumulative translation adjustments, investments in noncurrent marketable equity securities, certain investments of insurance companies, and pensions in determining whether a reporting entity should qualify for a deficit reclassification?**

The financial statements of a reporting entity may reflect positive retained earnings or a deficit in retained earnings and may have in addition separate components of equity resulting from:

o   The valuation allowance for noncurrent marketable equity securities (FASB Statements No. 12),

o   Net unrealized investment gains and losses of insurance companies (FASB Statement No. 60),

o   Cumulative translation adjustments (FASB Statement No. 52), or

o   Recording of an unfunded accumulated pension benefits obligation (FASB Statement No. 87).

Some believe a reporting entity with positive retained earnings should qualify for a deficit reclassification if its financial statements contain separate components of equity that would create a deficit in reported retained earnings were those items charged to retained earnings. They offer these reasons:

o   Such separate components of equity represent real economic detriments to a reporting entity's financial position at a point in time.

o   Because accumulated changes in the various separate components of equity are reported in equity, some users of financial statements may consider them together with retained earnings in evaluating a reporting entity's financial position.

o   FASB Concepts Statement No. 5 includes changes in the valuation allowance for noncurrent marketable equity securities and translation adjustments in comprehensive income.

Others believe that whether separate components of equity would create a deficit in reported retained earnings were they charged against retained earnings should not be considered in determining whether a reporting entity should qualify for a deficit reclassification. They offer these reasons:

o   In the absence of a deficit in reported retained earnings, the issue becomes whether to permit a procedure the purpose of which would be to eliminate the separate components of equity reported under FASB Statement Nos. 12, 52, 60, and 87. There is no basis in authoritative accounting literature or state corporation laws for such a procedure.

Further, it is unclear how such separate components of equity would be eliminated without either restating the balance sheet generally or changing (and at least complicating) the reporting in future periods for the kinds of transactions that give rise to the separate components of equity. For example, to report the subsequent realization of an unrealized gain by an insurance company in an income statement subsequent to a deficit reclassification, it would be necessary to charge paid in capital for the amount of the unrealized gain transferred to that account in the deficit reclassification.

o   Accumulated changes in the various separate components of equity are not in fact charged against retained earnings. What the balance in reported retained earnings might have been were accounting principles related to noncurrent marketable equity securities, certain investments of insurance companies, translation of foreign currency financial statements, and pensions different from what they are should not affect whether an entity should qualify for a deficit reclassification any more than what the balance in reported retained earnings might have been were other accounting principles different from what they are.

o Accumulated changes in the various separate components of equity probably do not impair reporting entities' ability to legally pay dividends.

A reverse situation would involve an entity with a deficit in retained earnings (and possibly debit balances in other separate components of equity) exceeded by a credit balance in a separate component of equity. The question would arise whether such an entity should qualify for a deficit reclassification, and the arguments would be similar to those above.

ISSUE 4: **Should a reporting entity have to have a substantial, factually supportable change in circumstances to qualify for a deficit reclassification?**

Some believe there should be a substantial, factually supportable change in circumstances, for example, a change in the line of business, marketing or operating philosophy, management personnel, equity control, or a legal reorganization to justify a deficit reclassification. Some believe a substantial contribution to capital by existing owners could also constitute a change in circumstances justifying a deficit reclassification.

Others believe a change in circumstances is merely an indication of a reporting entity's ability to achieve future profitability. They believe a change in circumstances should not be, in itself, a condition for allowing or disallowing a deficit reclassification.

ISSUE 5: **Should the deficit that is to be reclassified have to have resulted from net losses other than preoperating, start-up, or development stage losses?**

Some believe the deficit that is to be reclassified should have to have resulted principally from net losses other than preoperating, start-up, or development stage losses unless the reporting entity changes its business or changes the direction of its business and that change in direction is a change other than coming out of the preoperating, start-up, or development stage. They observe that application of generally accepted accounting principles generally results in the reporting of losses and accumulated deficits in such periods. They believe permitting reporting entities to reclassify deficits resulting solely from preoperating, start-up, or development stage losses would result in circumvention of current generally accepted accounting principles that are sound and accordingly would impair the usefulness of financial statements.

Others believe reporting entities should be permitted to reclassify deficits regardless of the causes of those deficits.

ISSUE 6 **Should the deficit to be reclassified have to have resulted principally from net losses and not from dividends or transactions involving the reporting entity's own stock?**

Some believe the deficit to be reclassified should have to have resulted principally from net losses and not from dividends or transactions involving the reporting entity's own stock. They believe the purpose of a deficit reclassification should be to provide relief to reporting entities that have suffered net losses, not to mitigate the financial reporting consequences of equity transactions or to facilitate such transactions.

Others who favor permitting a reporting entity to reclassify a deficit that resulted from dividends or transactions involving the reporting entity's own stock believe that an entity that could otherwise pay dividends, for example, when state law would permit dividends to be charged against unrealized appreciation in assets, should not be precluded from reclassifying its deficit.

ISSUE 7: **In the absence of a requirement in state law or the corporate charter for shareholder approval of a deficit reclassification, should a deficit**

reclassification have to be approved by a reporting entity's shareholders in order to be permitted?[5]

It is assumed that, if there is a requirement in state law or the corporate charter for shareholder approval of a deficit reclassification, shareholder approval would be obtained. (It is also assumed that the procedure would not be undertaken if it would violate existing debt covenants.) At issue, then, is whether deficit reclassifications for which shareholder approval is not required by state law or the corporate charter should be required to be approved by the reporting entity's shareholders in order to be permitted.

Some believe a deficit reclassification should have to be approved by a reporting entity's shareholders in order to be permitted. They observe that, unless a deficit reclassification is mandatory (see Issue 10), it is discretionary. They believe requiring shareholder approval of a deficit reclassification makes sure that shareholders approve of eliminating the deficit and will be aware that dividends paid after the deficit reclassification will be charged to retained earnings accumulated thereafter.

---

[5] A similar issue could be raised about requiring board of directors' approval in circumstances in which it is not required by law or corporate charter. The arguments for and against would be similar to those in this issue.

Also, they point out that ARB 43 requires shareholder approval for quasi-reorganizations.

Others believe that in the absence of a requirement in state law or the corporate charter for shareholder approval of a deficit reclassification, shareholder approval of a deficit reclassification should not be required. They argue that shareholder approval is not a precondition for using other accounting procedures and believe deficit reclassifications should not be singled out for such a requirement. They also argue that disclosure in the notes to the financial statements would adequately inform shareholders about the procedure.

ISSUE 8: **Should the separate financial statements of a wholly owned subsidiary be permitted to reflect a deficit reclassification if the parent company does not record its own deficit reclassification?**

Some believe that if a reporting entity is permitted to reclassify its deficit, by extension the same procedure should be permitted for a wholly owned subsidiary that is a separate reporting entity.

Others believe there is no need or reason for a deficit reclassification by a wholly owned subsidiary. They believe deficit reclassifications are directed primarily to shareholders, rather than to creditors or other user of financial statements. They point out that a parent company can obtain funds from its wholly owned subsidiary by means other than dividends and that eliminating a deficit will not affect the parent company's per-

134

ceptions of distributions made after a deficit reclassification or of its wholly owned subsidiary's financial position.

ISSUE 9: **Should a reporting entity be permitted to record a deficit reclassification more than once?**

Some believe a reporting entity should be permitted to record a deficit reclassification only once. They believe permitting a reporting entity to record a deficit reclassification more than once could result in manipulation of financial reporting.

Others believe that, because a corporate lifetime is indefinite, permitting only one deficit reclassification in a corporate lifetime is too severe a limitation. They would not preclude a deficit reclassification solely because the reporting entity had previously recorded one. Some would permit additional deficit reclassifications at any time but would require that the degree of justification for each additional deficit reclassification be greater than for the previous one, and some would permit additional deficit reclassifications only after reasonable intervals.

ISSUE 10: **Should a deficit reclassification ever be mandatory?**

Some believe a deficit reclassification should be solely voluntary. They believe a standard requiring deficit reclassifications in specified circumstances could not be written with sufficient clarity and precision to make sure the standard is applied uniformly.

Others believe a deficit reclassification should be discretionary unless the reporting entity undergoes a formal reorganization, in which case they believe it should be mandatory.

Still others believe a deficit reclassification should be mandatory if certain other events take place. Examples are a settlement with creditors, a troubled debt restructuring accompanied by owners' contribution of capital, and a significant change in a reporting entity's circumstances.

ISSUE 11: **Should reported retained earnings accumulated after a deficit reclassification be reasonably determinable in light of applicable state laws to support payment of dividends for a reporting entity to qualify for a deficit reclassification?**

Some believe that, for a reporting entity to qualify for a deficit reclassification, it should be reasonably determinable in light of applicable state laws that retained earnings accumulated after a deficit reclassification will support payment of dividends. They believe that a principal objective of deficit reclassification is to permit reporting entities that have the money and the desire to pay dividends to be permitted to do so and that, in the absence of a prospect of being permitted to pay dividends as a result of deficit reclassification, sufficient justification for the procedure does not exist.

136

Others believe the availability of reported retained earnings accumulated after a deficit reclassification for payment of dividends should not be a condition for permitting a deficit reclassification. They believe reporting entities should be permitted to reclassify their reported deficits in order to present their financial positions in a more favorable light.

Implementation Issues

Issue 12:   Should the separate accounts reported in equity that result from cumulative translation adjustments, investments in noncurrent marketable equity securities, certain investments of insurance companies, and pensions be eliminated in a deficit reclassification?

Issue 3 asked what consideration, if any, should be given to separate accounts reported in equity that result from cumulative translation adjustments, investments in noncurrent marketable equity securities, certain investments of insurance companies, and pensions in determining whether a reporting entity should qualify for a deficit reclassification. This issue asks whether those separate components of equity should be eliminated in a deficit reclassification, regardless of whether they were considered in determining whether a reporting entity should qualify for a deficit reclassification.

Some believe the separate components of equity should be eliminated in a deficit reclassification. They believe a deficit reclassification in which the separate components of equity are not eliminated is only a halfway measure.

Others believe the separate components of equity should not be eliminated in a deficit reclassification. They believe that if the separate components of equity are eliminated, accounting for subsequent changes in the related asset or liability accounts would produce results that were not intended in FASB Statement Nos. 12, 52, 60, and 87.

Post-Deficit Reclassification Issues

ISSUE 13: If the separate financial statements of a subsidiary reflect a deficit reclassification and the parent company does not record its own deficit reclassification, should the effects of the subsidiary's deficit reclassification be reversed in consolidation?

Some believe that if the separate financial statements of a subsidiary reflect a deficit reclassification and the parent company does not record its own deficit reclassification, the effects of the subsidiary's deficit reclassification should be reversed in consolidation. They compare deficit reclassifications recorded by subsidiaries to stock dividends declared by subsidiaries. ARB 51 states in that connection that

> Occasionally, subsidiary companies capitalize earned surplus arising since acquisition, by means of a stock dividend or otherwise. This does not require a transfer to capital surplus on consolidation, inasmuch as the retained earnings in the consolidated financial statements should

reflect the accumulated earnings of the consolidated group not distributed to the shareholders of, or capitalized by, the parent company.

Others believe such deficit reclassifications should not be reversed in consolidation; they believe the parent company's retained earnings should be increased by the amount of the deficit reclassified in the subsidiary's accounts.

ISSUE 14: **Should reported retained earnings be dated after a deficit reclassification?**

Some believe reported retained earnings should be dated after a deficit reclassification. They believe reported retained earnings ordinarily indicates the cumulative result of the reporting entity's earnings and dividends history. Dating puts users on notice that retained earnings is not such a cumulative result. Also, dating discloses that a deficit reclassification has been recorded and emphasizes the significance of the procedure.

Others believe dating reported retained earnings after a deficit reclassification creates an unnecessary stigma. They believe other disclosures would provide sufficient notice. Further, they observe that the reclassified deficit may have resulted from dividends paid during profitable periods or from other capital transactions.

Issues and Arguments

Part II - Accounting Reorganizations

Part II deals with quasi-reorganizations that result both in eliminating deficits and in restatements of assets or liabilities. Such quasi-reorganizations are referred to here as accounting reorganizations.

ISSUE 1: Should accounting reorganizations be permitted?

Some believe accounting reorganizations should be permitted. In their view, the disparity between the acquisition costs at which assets and liabilities are reported and their current fair values may be so great that financial statements are not meaningful. An accounting reorganization would enable a reporting entity to report assets, liabilities, and earnings of periods after the reorganization more satisfactorily.

Others believe accounting reorganizations should not be permitted. They offer these reasons:

o The literature supporting accounting reorganizations - ARB 43, Chapter 7A - is an anachronism. It predates the clean surplus theory adopted by APB Opinion 9, and, being discretionary, it lacks the discipline that mandatory standards provide.

o The current accounting model permits writing the costs of assets down only when the costs of assets are not recoverable. Though accounting for impairment of long-lived assets continues to be unsettled, an accounting reorganization could possibly permit a writedown that could not be otherwise justified. Moreover, as long as the requirement in APB 9 that adjustments made pursuant to a quasi-reorganization be excluded from the determination of net income is in place, an accounting reorganization would possibly permit an impairment or other writedown to bypass the income statement.[6]

o The realization principle prohibits writing assets up. Though there are acknowledged deficiencies in that principle, it is well understood and has stood the test of time. Accounting reorganizations should not be permitted to depart from that principle, particularly because it will be difficult to define with clarity and precision

---

[6] The FASB is considering a request from the AICPA that it address the accounting for the inability to recover fully the carrying amounts of long-lived assets, which was the subject of an AICPA issues paper.

the circumstances that would justify an accounting reorganization and thus the procedure may be largely discretionary.

Other arguments for and against permitting accounting reorganizations are essentially the same as the arguments in Issue 1 in Part I.

Conditions Under Which a Reporting Entity Should Be Permitted to Record an Accounting Reorganization

ISSUE 2:   If an accounting reorganization should be permitted, should there have to be a deficit in reported retained earnings to qualify for an accounting reorganization?

Some believe elimination of a deficit should be the principal objective of an accounting reorganization and therefore believe a deficit should be a precondition for an accounting reorganization.

Others believe allowing a reporting entity to make a fresh reporting start by cleansing the balance sheet of unrealistic reported amounts should be the principal objective of an accounting reorganization and therefore believe a deficit in retained earnings should not be a precondition for an accounting reorganization. Some believe an accounting reorganization should always follow a legal reorganization.

(If the answer to Issue 2 is "no," that would raise questions about the current accounting model that are beyond the scope of this paper. Accordingly, the remaining issues are based on the assumption that a deficit in reported retained earnings should be required to qualify for an accounting reorganization.)

ISSUE 3: If a deficit in retained earnings should be required in order for a reporting entity to qualify for an accounting reorganization, what consideration, if any, should be given to separate accounts reported in equity that result from cumulative translation adjustments, investments in noncurrent marketable equity securities, certain investments of insurance companies, and pensions?

Some believe a reporting entity with positive retained earnings should qualify for an accounting reorganization if its financial statements contain separate components of equity that would create a deficit in reported retained earnings were those items charged to retained earnings. They point out that the requirements for separate components of equity contained in FASB Statement Nos. 12, 52, 60, and 87 resulted from a desire to exclude those items from the income statement. Because accounting reorganizations are directed toward the balance sheet, income statement considerations should not determine whether a reporting entity should qualify for an accounting reorganization.

Others believe that whether separate components of equity would create a deficit in reported retained earnings were they charged against retained earnings should not be considered in determining whether a reporting entity should qualify for an accounting reorganization. They say that unrealized losses should not be considered to provide adequate proof of the need for such a radical accounting procedure.

Other arguments in this issue are essentially the same as the arguments in Issue 3 in Part I.

Also, the reverse situation described in Issue 3 in Part I, involving an entity with a deficit in retained earnings (and possibly debit balances in other separate components of equity) exceeded by a credit balance in a separate component of equity, would also apply to accounting reorganizations and the arguments would be similar to those above.

ISSUE 4:   If a deficit in retained earnings should be required in order for a reporting entity to qualify for an accounting reorganization, should the deficit have to have existed before the restatement of assets and liabilities?

Some believe a deficit should have to have existed before a restatement of assets and liabilities in an accounting reorganization, because they believe the principal objective of an accounting reorganization is to enable a reporting entity to pay dividends. Also, they point out that permitting reporting entities without deficits to qualify for accounting reorganizations if restatements of their assets would create deficits would encourage reporting entities to understate the amounts of their assets in the re-statement.

Others believe assets and liabilities should be re-stated to fair values and any resulting deficit eliminated because current and future operations should not be burdened with unrealistic reported amounts.

ISSUE 5:   Should a reporting entity demonstrate a reason-able prospect of future profitability to qualify for an accounting reorganization?

The arguments in this issue are essentially the same as the arguments in Issue 2 in Part I.

ISSUE 6:   Should a reporting entity have to have a substan-tial, factually supportable change in circumstan-ces to qualify for an accounting reorganization?

The arguments in this issue are essentially the same as the arguments in Issue 4 in Part I.

ISSUE 7:   Can the prospect of future profitability hinge on the new (presumably lower) bases of assets re-sulting from the accounting reorganization it-self?

Some believe the prospect of future profitability should be permitted to hinge on the new (presumably lower) bases of assets resulting from the accounting reorganization itself. They offer these reasons o   Those who would require a reporting entity to demonstrate a reasonable prospect of future profitability to qualify for an accounting reorganization would do so to avoid recurrence of a deficit in reported retained earnings. Future reported profits would avoid recurrence of a deficit regardless of the cause of those future profits.

o   New asset bases are more reliable than are many other matters as indicators of changes in future profitability.

o   Permitting the prospect of future profitability to hinge on new asset bases is consistent with the concept of a fresh start.

Others believe the prospect of future profitability should not be permitted to hinge on new asset bases, because they believe an accounting reorganization should be a response to a substantial, factually supportable change in circumstances and that a prospect of future profitability that hinges only on the accounting reorganization itself belies the existence of such a change in circumstances.

ISSUE 8:   **Should a reporting entity be permitted to record an accounting reorganization if total equity**

would be negative after the accounting reorganization?

Some believe the principal objective of an accounting reorganization should be to allow assets and liabilities to be reported satisfactorily and believe the prospect of continuing to report negative total equity after an accounting reorganization should not prevent more satisfactory reporting of assets and liabilities.

Others believe a reporting entity should not be permitted to record an accounting reorganization if negative total equity would remain after the accounting reorganization. They point out that such accounting reorganizations would contradict the idea of permitting a reporting entity to report the way it would were it starting fresh, because reporting entities do not start with negative total equity. They also point out that such accounting reorganizations would not permit payment of dividends, which some believe to be the principal objective of an accounting reorganization.

ISSUE 9: **Should a reporting entity be permitted to record an accounting reorganization if a deficit in retained earnings would remain after the accounting reorganization?**

The arguments in this issue are essentially the same as the arguments in Issue 8.

ISSUE 10: **Should reported retained earnings accumulated after an accounting reorganization be reasonably determinable in light of applicable state laws to support payment of dividends for a reporting**

entity to qualify for an accounting reorganization?

Some believe that for a reporting entity to qualify for an accounting reorganization, it should be reasonably determinable in light of applicable state laws that retained earnings accumulated after an accounting reorganization will support payment of dividends. They believe that a principal objective of accounting reorganizations is to permit reporting entities that have the money and the desire to pay dividends to be permitted to do so and that, in the absence of a prospect of being permitted to pay dividends as a result of an accounting reorganization, sufficient justification for the procedure does not exist.

Others believe enabling reporting entities to report assets, liabilities, and earnings of periods after the reorganization more satisfactorily is sufficient justification for the procedure. They believe deficiencies in the current accounting model make necessary a corrective mechanism for use when financial statements no longer satisfactorily portray the conditions and events they purport to portray. They believe financial reporting should not be governed by state laws that govern distributions to shareholders (for example, the laws of some states prohibit charging dividends against revaluation surplus) and believe maintaining separate accountability for dividend and financial reporting purposes would not cause reporting entities undue hardship and would not be misleading to users.

ISSUE 11: Should the deficit that justifies an accounting reorganization have to have resulted from net losses other than preoperating, start-up, or development stage losses?

The arguments in this issue are essentially the same as the arguments in Issue 5 in Part I.

ISSUE 12: Should the deficit that justifies an accounting reorganization have to have resulted principally from net losses and not from dividends or transactions involving the reporting entity's own stock?

The arguments in this issue are essentially the same as the arguments in Issue 6 in Part I.

ISSUE 13: Should a reporting entity whose reported equity is believed to be understated because application of generally accepted accounting principles results in assets being reported at less than their current fair values or liabilities being reported at more than their current fair values be precluded from recording an accounting reorganization?

Some object to permitting reporting entities whose reported equity is believed to be understated because application of generally accepted accounting principles results in the assets being reported at less than their current fair values or liabilities being reported at more than their current fair values to record accounting reorganizations. Whether an accounting reorganization would result in a net increase in equity depends on how a number of subsequent issues are resolved, including what assets should be restated, how those assets should be restated, whether any or all liabilities should be restated, and whether restatement should be based on the values of identifiable assets and liabilities or on a valuation of the entity as a whole. This Issue 13 is therefore a threshold issue, dealing with whether a reporting entity whose reported equity is believed to be understated should be precluded from recording an accounting reorganization regardless of the accounting rules that will be devised. If it should not be so precluded, Issue 22 addresses whether adjustments in the reorganization should be limited so that there is no increase in equity.

Those who object to permitting reporting entities whose reported equity is believed to be understated to record accounting reorganizations believe that it would contradict the idea of a troubled entity that is implicit in the concept of an accounting reorganization. Also, they believe the reasons for restatement of assets and liabilities are to recognize currently the excess of the amounts at which assets are stated over their current fair values so that future earnings will not be burdened with that excess and to prevent the need for future accounting reorganizations. Only accounting reorganizations of entities whose reported equity is overstated are consistent with that belief.

Others believe the fact that a reporting entity's reported equity is believed to be understated should not preclude it from reporting its assets and liabilities more satisfactorily.

ISSUE 14: Should the separate financial statements of a

subsidiary be permitted to reflect an accounting reorganization if the parent company does not record its own accounting reorganization?

The arguments in this issue are essentially the same as the arguments in Issue 8 in Part I.

ISSUE 15: In the absence of a requirement in state law or the corporate charter for shareholder approval of an accounting reorganization, should an accounting reorganization have to be approved by a reporting entity's shareholders in order to be permitted?

It is assumed that, if there is a requirement in state law or the corporate charter for shareholder approval of an accounting reorganization, shareholder approval would be obtained. (It is also assumed that the procedure would not be undertaken if it would violate existing debt covenants.) At issue, then, is whether accounting reorganizations for which shareholder approval is not required by state law or the corporate charter should be required to be approved by the reporting entity's shareholders in order to be permitted.

The arguments in this issue are essentially the same as the arguments in Issue 7 in Part I. However, those who believe an accounting reorganization should have to be approved by a reporting entity's shareholders in order to be permitted offer as an additional consideration the radicalness of the procedure which, they emphasize, is discretionary (assuming that Issue 17 is answered "no").

ISSUE 16: **Should a reporting entity be permitted to record an accounting reorganization more than once?**

The arguments in this issue are essentially the same as the arguments in Issue 9 in Part I.

ISSUE 17: **Should an accounting reorganization ever be mandatory in circumstances other than those described in Issue 32?**

The arguments in this issue are essentially the same as the arguments in Issue 10 in Part I.

Accounting Procedures

ISSUE 18: **Should all identifiable assets be restated in an accounting reorganization?**

Some believe only assets for which there is evidence of impairment should be restated. They believe the purpose of an accounting reorganization is to permit a reporting entity to avoid having future results of operations burdened by charges that do not result from earning activities that benefit its operations commensurately. Under this view, restatement is applied only to significant assets that would otherwise result in such future charges.

Some would focus on major classes of assets and would restate all the assets in a class provided the net effect was to reduce the carrying amount of the class; for example, of three buildings owned by a reporting entity, two might require reduction whereas the value of the third exceeds its carrying amount.

Others believe an accounting reorganization should permit a reporting entity to report as though it is starting fresh and that requires a comprehensive restatement of assets. They believe a comprehensive restatement is a feature that distinguishes an accounting reorganization from a writedown of assets to reflect impairment. In their view, permitting selective restatement would be far too discretionary.

ISSUE 19: **Should liabilities be restated in an accounting reorganization?**

Some believe liabilities should be restated in an accounting reorganization. They believe restating liabilities is consistent with the idea of permitting a reporting entity to report the way it would were it starting fresh. They also point out that liabilities (usually monetary) should be more susceptible of objective restatement than nonmonetary assets.

Others believe liabilities should not be restated in an accounting reorganization. They point out that ARB 43 does not suggest restatement of liabilities. They also point out that if liabilities were restated to their fair values, that would typically result in credits to equity because of financial difficulties of the reporting entity.

Still others believe that only some liabilities should be

restated.   They note, however, that FASB Statement No. 15 might apply when a troubled debt restructuring coincides with an accounting reorganization unless "the debtor restates its liabilities generally."

ISSUE 20: Should the restatement be based on the values of identifiable assets and liabilities or should it be based on a valuation of the reporting entity as a whole?

Some believe the reporting entity should ideally be valued as a whole; the value of all the reporting entity's common stock should be determined and amounts should be assigned to assets and liabilities, including possibly goodwill, as would be done in a business combination accounted for by the purchase method under APB Opinion 16. They argue that, if the value of a reporting entity's stock is a reasonable basis for reporting assets and liabilities in a business combination accounted for by the purchase method, it is a reasonable basis for restatement of assets and liabilities in an accounting reorganization. They also argue that an equity infusion, which may accompany an accounting reorganization, could provide evidence of value of the entire enterprise and may include a payment for existing goodwill.   They also believe that, if unidentifiable intangibles constitute a significant portion of a company's value, they should not be ignored in an accounting reorganization. Further, goodwill (unidentified intangibles) can exist in any business enterprise; its existence should not be ignored in an accounting procedure that purports to restate all assets to fair values.

Others believe only identifiable assets, tangible and intangible, and liabilities should be restated. They offer the following reasons for that position:

o Valuation is not an exact science, and, in the absence of a purchase transaction or a significant equity infusion, there would undoubtedly be more difficulty in valuing a reporting entity as a whole than in restating individual assets and liabilities.

o Though market prices may exist for some of a reporting entity's stock, there are no market prices available for all of a reporting entity's stock. An accounting reorganization can be distinguished from a business combination accounted for by the purchase method in which stock is the consideration and the value of the stock is the basis for accounting by the purchase method. The amount of stock of the acquiring company issued in the combination is typically less than the amount of the acquiring company's stock already outstanding.

o Reporting goodwill would contradict the idea of permitting a reporting entity to report the way

it would were it starting fresh, because there is
no goodwill when buying individual new assets to
form a new entity. Reporting goodwill also con-
tradicts the idea of a troubled entity that is
implicit in an accounting reorganization.

o Valuing equity varies too drastically from the
acquisition cost basis unless it is accompanied,
as a separate consideration, by an application of
pushdown accounting resulting from a major change
in ownership.

o There is little support in ARB 43 and little, if
any, in practice for revaluation of the entity as
a whole.

Still others would base the restatement on the value of
the entity as a whole if such value is clearly determinable, and
on the value of identifiable assets and liabilities if the value
of the entity as a whole is not clearly determinable.

ISSUE 21: Should amounts be assigned to individual assets
and liabilities in accordance with the guidelines
in paragraph 88 of APB Opinion 16, or should
amounts be assigned to individual assets and
liabilities another way?

Some believe individual assets and liabilities that are to
be revalued should be stated at fair values, because they believe

that is most consistent with the concept of a fresh start. They would use the guidelines in paragraph 88 of APB Opinion 16 to determine those fair values, because those guidelines are widely used and well understood.

Others favor stating assets at the amounts of the net future cash flows those assets are expected to generate.

Still others would discount the net future cash flows or would otherwise derive amounts that would allow profit to be reported on the sale or use of those assets. They believe that the concept of recoverable amount or of value in use to the enterprise, as used in FASB Statement No. 33, is useful. Opponents of such methods argue that it is difficult if not impossible to predict future cash flows to be generated by assets and to attribute estimated future cash flows to individual assets, that interactions among assets make the procedure meaningless, that the choice of a discount rate, at least with respect to nonmonetary items, is too subjective, and that predictions do not belong in historical reports.

ISSUE 22: If a reporting entity whose recorded equity is believed to be understated because application of generally accepted accounting principles results in the assets being recorded at less than their current fair values or liabilities being recorded at more than their current fair values is permitted to record an accounting reorganization, should assets and liabilities be restated only to the extent that the restatement would not cause an increase in equity?

Issue 13 discusses whether a reporting entity whose recorded equity is believed to be understated because application of generally accepted accounting principles results in the assets being recorded at less than their current fair values or liabilities being recorded at more than their current fair values should be precluded from recording an accounting reorganization. This issue discusses whether, if such an entity is not precluded from recording an accounting reorganization, adjustments in the reorganization should be limited so that there is no net increase in equity.

The limitation is proposed by those who believe that reporting entities whose reported equity is believed to be understated should not be precluded from recording accounting reorganizations, but they believe that the reorganization should not result in a net increase in equity. They argue that restatements that result in increases in equity would deviate too much from the prohibitions against appraisal write ups in current GAAP. They observe that, in industries such as real estate, for which it is often asserted that current value financial statements are more relevant than financial statements based on acquisition costs, such restatements could permit introduction of current values into financial statements prepared in conformity with generally accepted accounting principles that are otherwise precluded. While they might agree that current values are more relevant in such industries, they believe that accounting reorganizations should not be the means to achieve that result.

In determining whether an accounting reorganization results in a net increase in equity for this purpose, some would consider associated writedowns due to impairment or other losses charged to income in the same or a proximate reporting period.

Others believe that the limitation is inconsistent with permitting a reporting entity to report as if it is starting fresh. They believe that assets and liabilities should be restated to the same extent that they would be were a new corporation created and that corporation acquired the assets and liabilities of the existing corporation. They point out that accounting reorganizations sometimes accompany bankruptcy proceedings and that, in such proceedings, creditors often agree to significantly reduce obligations under debt agreements. They further observe that the application of FASB Statement No. 15 to such debt restructurings may preclude recognizing in the period of restructuring the concessions made by the creditors and may, in the absence of an accounting reorganization that increases equity by writing the restructured debt down to its current value, preclude emergence from bankruptcy with positive equity. They also believe the limitation would require that an arbitrary procedure be specified for putting the limitation into effect; they observe that at least some assets or liabilities would not be restated to fair values. They further question the usefulness of an accounting reorganization that does not affect equity but only reallocates carrying amounts of assets and liabilities.

Still others believe that restatements of assets that must be written down by a charge to income under generally accepted accounting principles should be distinguished from restatements that are discretionary and that are permitted only on the basis of an accounting reorganization. They believe net discretionary restatements in an accounting reorganization should not be permitted to result in a net increase in equity.

Issue 23: Should the separate accounts reported in equity that result from cumulative translation adjustments, investments in noncurrent marketable equity securities, certain investments of insurance companies, and pensions be eliminated in an accounting reorganization?

Some believe that the separate accounts reported in equity that result from cumulative translation adjustments, noncurrent marketable equity securities, certain investments of insurance companies, and pensions should be eliminated in an accounting reorganization. They point out that the requirements for separate components of equity in FASB Statement Nos. 12, 52, 60, and 87 resulted from a desire to exclude those items from the income statement and at the same time to adhere to the clean surplus theory in APB Opinion 9. Given the radical nature of accounting reorganizations, neither excluding those items from income nor adhering to the clean surplus theory should be a significant consideration in deciding how the balance sheet should appear after an accounting reorganization. The amounts reported as separate components of equity are, stated broadly, amounts that will eventually be cleared to income. (Of course, they may also be reversed if, for example, unrealized appreciation or depreciation of equity securities is eliminated by market price changes.) An accounting reorganization provides a fresh start, a new balance sheet from which to measure future results. Accordingly, amounts lodged in separate components of equity at the date of the accounting reorganization should not be reflected in future income statements and should be eliminated in the accounting reorganization.

Others believe the separate accounts reported in equity should not be eliminated in an accounting reorganization. They believe accounting reorganizations should be directed at the reporting entities' assets and liabilities, not at the classification of the residual amounts that result from those assets and liabilities. Further, they argue that the separate accounts reported in equity are required by authoritative literature and that that literature should not be disregarded.

Other arguments in this issue are similar to those in Issue 3 in Part I and to Issue 3 in Part II.

ISSUE 24: Should accumulated depreciation and amortization be eliminated when restating assets in an accounting reorganization?

Some believe that to write depreciable or amortizable assets up or down, their acquisition costs should be left intact and only accumulated depreciation or amortization should be adjusted. They believe the resulting financial statement presentation is more informative.

Others believe accumulated depreciation and amortization should be eliminated and the related assets adjusted to the intended amounts. They believe that approach is consistent with the concept of a fresh start.

ISSUE 25: **Should an accounting reorganization result in a new reporting entity?**

Some believe an accounting reorganization, which is based on the concept of a fresh start, creates a new reporting entity and that financial statements following the accounting reorganization should be those of the new reporting entity. They observe that the accounting reorganization destroys comparability of prereorganization and postreorganization financial statements, and they believe that it follows that postreorganization financial statements are those of a new reporting entity. They believe pro forma financial information should be presented for periods before the accounting reorganization as it is in business combinations accounted for by the purchase method; such information would reflect the values assigned in the reorganization. They also believe historical financial statements should, if presented, be considered those of a predecessor entity. Creating a new reporting entity would eliminate the issue of whether to include the restatement adjustment in income, but it would raise other issues, not dealt with in this issues paper, such as whether the accounting policies for the new reporting entity should be allowed to be selected or changed without concern for preferability.

Others believe that, because the reporting entity after the accounting reorganization is the same legal and economic entity it was before the accounting reorganization, treating the reporting entity in financial statements following the accounting reorganization as a new reporting entity would mislead. They believe it should be enough to label results of operations as before and after the accounting reorganization.

ISSUE 26: **If an accounting reorganization does not result in creating a new reporting entity and the restatement adjustment results in a net decrease in recorded equity, should the adjustment be reported in income?**

Some believe a restatement that results in a net decrease in recorded equity should be reported in income. They offer the all-inclusive (clean surplus) theory of income determination, described in APB 9, as support for their position.

Others believe the restatement adjustment should be reported as a direct charge or credit to equity. They view an accounting reorganization as directed toward the balance sheet and believe the income statement would be more meaningful if unencumbered by its effects. However, they believe that if the restatement adjustment would ordinarily be reported in income under GAAP, for example, a writedown or writeoff due to impairment of land, buildings, and equipment used in the business, equipment leased to others, or goodwill, it should be reported in the income statement for the period preceding the reorganization. Accounting reorganizations should not be used to avoid charges to income.

Proponents of reflecting the adjustment directly in equity observe that FASB Concepts Statement No. 5 establishes separate concepts of earnings and comprehensive income and believe net adjustments arising in accounting reorganizations might properly be excluded from earnings.

ISSUE 27: **If an accounting reorganization does not result in creating a new reporting entity and the restatement adjustment results in a net increase in recorded equity, should the adjustment be reported in income?**

Some believe that, if adjustments that result in net decreases in recorded equity are included in income, restatement adjustments that result in increases in recorded equity should also be included in income. They base that view on the concept of neutrality in financial reporting.

Others believe restatement adjustments that result in increases in recorded equity should be included in income only to the extent they offset asset write downs or other losses charged to income in the same or a proximate reporting period.

Still others believe restatement adjustments that result

in increases in recorded equity should never be included in income. They believe including such restatement adjustments in income would deviate from the prohibition against including unrealized profits in income in ARB 43, Chapter 1A.

ISSUE 28: **If the restatement adjustment should be reported in income, should it be reported as an extraordinary item?**

Some believe that if the restatement adjustment should be reported in income, it should be reported as an extraordinary item. They believe income before extraordinary items should represent the results of a reporting entity's customary business activities and believe including the restatement adjustment in income before extraordinary items would impair the ability of the income statement to help users make predictions as the basis for decisions.

Others believe that if the restatement adjustment should be reported in income, it should be included in income before extraordinary items. They believe that, though the adjustment may meet the criterion in APB Opinion 30 that extraordinary items be infrequent, it would not meet the criterion that extraordinary items be unusual, that is, of a character significantly different from the typical or customary business activities of the entity. Further, they believe that the restatement adjustment may be largely indistinguishable from an impairment writedown and, consequently, they believe the entire restatement adjustment should be included in income before extraordinary items. Moreover, they believe there is no reason to exclude the restatement adjustment from income before extraordinary items. They believe the ability of the income statement to help users make predictions as the basis for decisions would not be impaired by including the adjustment in income before extraordinary items, because the current period's income statement will have little such ability after the accounting reorganization in any event.

Post Accounting Reorganization Issues

ISSUE 29: If an accounting reorganization (1) results in a new reporting entity or (2) does not result in a new reporting entity and the restatement adjustment is not reported in income, how should changes made after an accounting reorganization to amounts assigned to assets and liabilities in an accounting reorganization be presented?

Amounts assigned to assets and liabilities in an accounting reorganization sometimes are changed after the accounting reorganization, because management decides those amounts are unsatisfactory. For example, the stated amount of an asset that reflects an estimate of the cost to dispose of that asset might be changed before the asset is disposed of if it appears that the cost to dispose of the asset will differ substantially from the previously estimated cost, or an asset or liability that was not recorded in an accounting reorganization might subsequently be seen to have existed at the time of the accounting reorganization.

Similarly, disposition of an asset or settlement of a liability at an amount different from that assigned to it in the accounting reorganization results in a gain or loss, which may be deemed to be an adjustment of the amount assigned to the asset or liability in the accounting reorganization. The question is whether such changes should be reflected in income of the post accounting reorganization period or whether they should be used to adjust the amounts assigned in the accounting reorganization. If the latter, the adjustments would be reflected directly in equity if the accounting reorganization is based on identifiable assets and liabilities (Issue 20) and if the accounting reorganization is based on valuation of the entity as a whole, would be used to adjust the allocation to individual assets and liabilities of the value of the entity as a whole. (It is assumed that there would be general agreement that if the accounting reorganization does not result in a new reporting entity and the restatement adjustment is reported in income, post reorganization changes would also be reflected in income, and that therefore there is no issue to address that circumstance.) This issue does not address tax loss carryforwards or investment tax credit carryforwards.

Some believe such changes in stated amounts of assets and liabilities should be reflected in income in the years they are made, because they believe those changes reflect changes in economic circumstances subsequent to the accounting reorganization. In their view, it is not practical after the passage of time to determine whether a revaluation represents an improvement in an estimate or a change due to changed circumstances.

Others believe such changes in stated amounts of assets and liabilities should be excluded from income only if they are made within a specified period of time after the accounting reorganization. They believe such changes are similar to changes in allocations of purchase prices of acquired enterprises that result from resolution of preacquisition contingencies, such as settlements of litigation pending at acquisition dates. FASB Statement No. 38 states that if preacquisition contingencies assumed in business combinations accounted for by the purchase method are resolved within an allocation period, usually not to exceed one year, they should be included in the purchase allocation and that otherwise they should be included in the determination of net income.

Still others believe that all such changes in stated amounts of assets and liabilities should be reflected directly in equity. They believe the income statement would be more meaningful if unencumbered by items related to the accounting reorganization. Further, they observe that if changes to amounts assigned in the accounting reorganization are reflected in income, there may be an incentive to assign values that will result in post accounting reorganization credits.

For assets to be disposed of after the accounting reorganization, some believe changes in stated amounts should be reflected in income unless disposal of the assets was planned at the time of the accounting reorganization.

Some believe that how such changes should be presented may depend on whether assets and liabilities should be restated individually in an accounting reorganization or whether amounts assigned to assets and liabilities should be based on a revaluation of the reporting entity as a whole.

ISSUE 30: **Should reported retained earnings be dated after an accounting reorganization?**

The arguments in this issue are essentially the same as the arguments in Issue 14 in Part I.

ISSUE 31: **If the separate financial statements of a subsidiary reflect an accounting reorganization and the parent company does not record its own accounting reorganization, should the effects of the subsidiary's accounting reorganization be reversed in consolidation?**

Some believe that if the separate financial statements of a subsidiary reflect an accounting reorganization and the parent company does not record its own accounting reorganization, the effects of the subsidiary's accounting reorganization should be reversed in consolidation. They offer these reasons:

o Not reversing in consolidation the effects of a subsidiary's accounting reorganization would constitute, in effect, a partial accounting reorganization of the consolidated group. They be-

lieve partial accounting reorganizations should
not be permitted.

o The consolidated group likely has not met the
requisite conditions for an accounting reorganization (assuming the procedure is not completely
discretionary).

o Not reversing in consolidation the effects of a
subsidiary's accounting reorganization would constitute an unjustified departure from the acquisition cost basis.

Others believe that if the separate financial statements
of a subsidiary reflect an accounting reorganization and the
parent company does not record its own accounting reorganization,
the effects of the subsidiary's accounting reorganization should
be reflected in the consolidated financial statements. They
offer these reasons:

o The consolidated financial statements should
reflect the same amounts for the subsidiary as
are reflected in the subsidiary's financial
statements.

o The subsidiary's accounting reorganization may
provide sufficient evidence of a loss of value to

the parent company to permit the parent company to write down its investment in the subsidiary.

ISSUE 32: If consolidated financial statements reflect an accounting reorganization of the parent company, should the parent company's accounting reorganization be pushed down to the separate financial statements of its wholly owned subsidiary or subsidiaries?

Some believe that if consolidated financial statements reflect an accounting reorganization of the parent company, the reorganization should be pushed down to the separate financial statements of its wholly owned subsidiaries. They believe the subsidiaries' separate financial statements should reflect the same amounts as are reflected for the subsidiaries in the consolidated financial statements. They further observe that, when the subsidiaries have met the requisite conditions for recording accounting reorganizations, whether the subsidiaries record their own accounting reorganizations is likely a matter of the parent company's discretion, and they believe permitting the parent company discretion in such cases could result in manipulation of financial reporting. Finally, they point to the trend in practice toward more frequent push down to the subsidiary's financial statements of APB 16 purchase accounting adjustments.

Others believe a parent company's accounting reorganization should not be pushed down to its subsidiaries' separate financial statements. They point out that the subsidiaries may not have met the requisite conditions for recording accounting reorganizations. They also point out that, even if the subsidiaries meet the requisite conditions, accounting reorganizations are discretionary and that the subsidiaries have not chosen to record accounting reorganizations. They further point out that pushing a parent company's accounting reorganization down to the separate financial statements of its subsidiaries without the formal approval of the subsidiaries' directors or shareholders may conflict with provisions of state laws governing distributions to shareholders. They are also concerned that there might be circumstances--for example, a subsidiary is regulated or has debt held by third parties--that would further suggest that the parent company's accounting reorganization should not be pushed down to its subsidiaries' separate financial statements.

Those opposing pushing down an accounting reorganization point out the absence of the circumstances in an accounting reorganization that argue for push down accounting in a business combination accounted for by the purchase method--a transaction at arm's length that provides objective evidence of the value of the subsidiary and one that typically involves only the subsidiary whose financial statements give rise to the push down accounting question. Further, the assets and liabilities of the subsidiary may be carried at different amounts in the subsidiary's separate statements and in consolidation if the subsidiary was acquired in a purchase business combination in which push down accounting was not applied. There could be various implementation difficulties, for example, the amount **and even** the direction (write up or write down) of the net **adjustment** to equity could be different.